The

Bliss & Blues of TV News!

The Ten Terrible Truths
of
Television News

By Gene Minshall

Thumbs Up Publishing

Cover Design: Ben Gallegos

ISBN 978-0-9840572-6-9

Thumbs Up Publishing

Franklin, TN. 37064

The Bliss & Blues of TV News

By Gene Minshall

Thumbs Up Publishing

Cover Design: Ben Gallegos

ISBN 978-0-9840572-6-9

Thumbs Up Publishing

Franklin, TN. 37064

Copyright © Minshall 2013

Printed in the United States and Europe.

CONTENTS

Introduction   5

Preface   11

1. News is a monster, impossible to totally control and as changeable in definition as a drifting cloud in an open sky..........................   17

2. If local TV newscasts suddenly ceased to exist, life, as we know it, wouldn't skip a beat........................   34

3. You can be absolutely accurate in the information you present, and dead wrong in the impression you leave......................   54

4. Contrary to its own marketing, a local TV newscast is not the voice of the people or even an accurate reflection of the community........................   73

5. You cannot judge a Television news operation by its promotion   98

6. More than journalistic integrity, spectacular production techniques and wide-ranging coverage---it is the Anchor who carries a station's news image........................   122

7. Television is a triumph of equipment over people   136

8. Flashing red lights illuminate the stage of a local TV news operation........................   149

9. An ordinary picture takes precedence over the most profoundly written word........................   173

10. TV News loves to misbehave, opting for controversy over substance, image over reality, and never letting a story die..................   184

A Parting Shot 208

Introduction

Shaw had a lot to say about a lot of things. He particularly seemed to take issue with what was written by journalists in general, though he was a writer of extraordinary skill himself. Journalists can, indeed, make the biggest fuss over the most trivial happening. They did then and they do now. When a TV news crew happens to shoot spectacular tape of an ordinary event, you can bet your front row tickets at Armageddon that the TV station will exert two to three times more effort on the story than it deserves, and a story that realistically affects the viewer in some way may be ignored or get only a brief mention. Watching every newscast everyday one would think that civilization *is* collapsing; shootings, accidents, disasters and continuing crime are part of the landscape, not to mention oil spills, floods, wars, miners trapped for months, an unstable economy and the rising cost of tickets at Disneyland. To an alien, visiting this planet, with only a newscast for information, he would probably get back on his ship, take a Valium, and get as far away from earth as possible.

Who left a white Armani garment bag at the Delta ticket counter?
Announcement over the Chicago's O'Hare Airport loudspeaker

I heard that announcement while sitting at a lunch counter in the O'Hare airport. People around me all looked up. Some smiled, a few shook their heads, and others said something to the stranger beside them. Perhaps all were curious about the person who could walk off and leave an Armani garment bag behind. What evoked the public reaction? Certainly not that a garment bag was left at a ticket counter; that happens every day at O'Hare without so much as a glance or a snicker. Obviously, what caused a momentary hesitation with O'Hare's travelers was the fact that it was a *white Armani* bag. A purple cow couldn't have drawn more attention. In a strange way, this is a part of what every news department in every city in every state tries to do; grab the viewers as quickly as possible, use a familiar name to attract attention, entice them with an unusual or tantalizing line and give them a reason to stay with a particular station for fear of missing something…and come back another night for more of the same.

When the visual isn't available, the written word will have to do. Admittedly flashing red lights have a way of grabbing your attention and holding it until there is a reason to look elsewhere; mere words *can* have an equal impact, if they are given the chance. The problem is most TV news departments don't believe it; too often, they just let the picture do the talking. This is one of the terrible truths.

My job is not to be like today's news trendsetters but rather one who observes and comments…all from experience, reading, watching, and talking with journalists of all occasion. The Ten Terrible Truths didn't just happen; they evolved over the years—with too many people still unaware of their existence. I was part of that evolution, watching and listening to everyone from John Cameron Swayze with fuzzy and dated visuals to Brian Williams with live reports from around the world, not to the mention the gee-whiz graphics that reinforces the information. It's been quite a ride.

The Ten Terrible Truths of Television News, is not meant to imply that newscasts don't have merit; quite the contrary. Some news is highly professional and serve great purposes of description and explanation of events in the community, as well as those lighthearted moments that also sustain us. A *Terrible Truth*, on the other hand, is just something we have learned to live with—sometimes unbalanced, unfair, unnecessary, biased *or* even painfully right on the mark. Some are even refreshingly presented and accepted. But mostly, it points out the inequities and imperfections of the industry. Given the perplexing task of trying to define *news* in the first place, the term *Terrible Truths* only complicates the assignment of daily informing a viewing audience. A fact, among all the terrible truths is that each one is part of the other. While I try not to make judgments on whether the terrible truths are right or wrong, I freely express opinion, lament some of the practices and ask questions.

Some opening notes to consider…

Our world is in turmoil and crisis. People are struggling as never before, trying to cope with everything from disputes on foreign soil to a neighborhood ordinance that is causing local dissention. Further, questionable practices and agendas seem to be around every corner. The first steps to understanding and bringing ultimate resolution begin with acquiring information, being aware of what is happening in the community and state, and being informed enough to ask the right questions before making important decisions. Amazingly, we are blitzed by information. Magazines, the Internet, a glut of newspapers and information-based television programs are available to everyone—yet people make some of their most critical decisions with the slightest, unconfirmed information. But that's only part of the problem.

Rosa Brooks, law professor at the Georgetown U. Law Center, has said that the "*yapping heads who dominate cable news,*" triggers in most people that one element that both compromises and complicates a viewer's sense of being well informed: *opinion*. Never before has there been so much comment and criticism on issues that influence our lives. The simple straightforward reporting of an event or an entity is no longer the norm. The airwaves are filled with someone taking a shot at some individual or incident and do it with such conviction that too often a viewer's opinion is firmly formed instead of thinking for himself and checking all the available news sources. The problem with "opinion" is that it is long on *talk* and short on *solutions*.

It should be remembered that the glut of radio and TV commentators—Limbaugh, Hannity, and Beck among them—are expressing opinion on the news *and not reporting the unfolding news itself, (though Fox network tries to do both*.) Listeners and viewers with no opinions, or at least an opinion with little or nothing to back it up, lick up this available comment like it was frosting left on the side of the mixing bowl. It's enough information to taste the flavor of an opinion but not enough to make a sound and rational judgment. Considering the individual pressures people face every day, coupled with their fading interest in current events, it is hardly a mystery that they don't know more about their world…and *why*—almost without question—would they allow a few to speak for the many, while industries from banking to health care prey upon the vulnerability of their clients. There is enough information out there to assist people in making decisions and not passively letting the selfish, the unqualified, the egoists, the ignorant, the imposters, the greedy, the overtly aggressive, and the opinionated making choices that directly affect *our* lives.

It's no wonder problems don't get solved; corporate greed runs rampant, government is suspect, school drop-outs are at an all time high and families are dissolving at an alarming rate. It is a cliché to say that there are no easy answers. But responsible people and organizations, given the right tools, techniques and accurate information, *can* slowly make a difference. The obvious and most effective means is through the communications industry. But changes will have to be made. The challenge is twofold: to get the people to *listen, read and watch. (*Right now, more people have to be convinced that the media actually *have* information they can use.) And secondly …use *courage, creativity and an unprecedented zeal* in presenting that information. This, however, would necessitate new tactics and a new attitude.

We can go in a dozen different directions but for the purpose of this book, we'll concentrate on television news. This most extreme dimension of all journalism has one of the better chances to be of greater value to the people-at-large, to inform and engage those who are ready to receive information that might assist them to better understand the world around them and the community next to them. Journalists are in a position—and television is the perfect delivery system—to convey information to people who are looking for answers. They want to know what is going on with their government. Further, they want an accurate overview of their community and an explanation of the daily unfolding of events. Simply, they are looking for a break to help hold life and limb together for another day. But there's a problem …

Neglect is a thread that weaves its way through every newscast every day and night. Too many reporters are falling short of their duties while playing fast and loose with the intelligence and patience of their viewers. Though, some reporters can be absolutely brilliant—bringing honor to their profession—too many are lazy and uncommitted. They are squandering their God given talents with a crash, boom, bang attitude & approach and ignore a chance to be a beacon of *light and reason* for the viewers. And they are guided by management and consultants obsessed with ratings and budgets. Almost every night viewers have a choice of videos that show a fire—in or out of control, flashing red lights, yellow police tape flapping in the wind, live shots with reporters standing in the rain—with or without an umbrella—a car chase and a resulting crash, and excited eyewitnesses who have little or nothing to add to a story. And sometimes you might see it all in a single night while neglecting what is truly important in people's lives.

Sadly, ending our day by seeing the worst of mankind and what happens when safety and caution are ignored is hardly a formula for a positive frame of mind when your head hits the pillow. Psychologists give us more to chew on when they tell us that being consistently bombarded with negative images also determines human behavior and reinforces an indifference and helplessness toward positive action. The news departments of TV stations still seem to approach the lead stories of crime, crashes and controversy with an intensity that rivals the appearance of the bubonic plague in our neighborhoods.

Fortunately, most of those highly negative stories affect only a visceral, *not* a realistic level of the viewer, because as suddenly as they appear, they are gone and forgotten. Conversely, a station's promotion department always shouts out the virtues of the news department, how it informs, educates, guides and helps people make important decisions in their lives, never mentioning that 50% of the news is composed of crime and accidents, leaving only a few minutes for everything else that has happened that day. And yes, of course, there are stories of crime and accidents that are very important to the community and need to be right up front on a newscast, but only rarely. Most of the time, the idea seems to be to pander to the viewer while robbing him of his right to be better informed on issues to which he can relate.

Increasingly, the sane and insane are given equal time to spread their gospel, blurring the lines of difference between the preposterous and the practical. While there are times when there is a reference to a particular station or network in this book, there is cohesion that all share. Studies by an independent group, funded by PEW and their "Excellence in Journalism" projects have found that TV news operations from coast to coast and border to border have common denominators that can confuse and frustrate. Granted, reference may be made to a particular story in Denver but it is not unlike an event in Minneapolis, Atlanta, Fresno, Buffalo or Fargo. *Terrible Truths* in one city present the same challenges and carry the same burdens, in varying sizes, in every other news operation. The industry, even in the midst of an uncertain economy, still has an enormous obligation to keep the people informed *and* make money for the stockholders and keeping stations on the air. Doing both is a magic trick worthy of Houdini on his best day; on his worst day, one side will suffer. Hint: it won't be the stockholders.

To the viewer, it must be stated that TV news cannot *solve* a problem, nor is that its intent, but what it can do is *identify* the problem and what is or isn't being done about it. And it can give voice to those events, large and small, that give rise to opportunity and optimism.

This is a book that has been simmering for a long time.

Preface

In tackling this subject and because a journalist or two will be reading it, I am reminded of a story told to me by a friend, Neal Maxwell. He related the tale of the man who survived the Johnstown flood. He spent the remaining years of his life cornering everyone he could to tell them how he struggled and eventually survived the raging waters. The event became his consuming passion. After he passed on, he encountered St. Peter at the entrance to Heaven who told him that his good and decent life had earned him the right to have one wish fulfilled upon his entrance. Excitedly, the man told St. Peter that he would like to have a gathering of heavenly hosts so that he could tell them how he survived the Johnstown flood. St. Peter said that he could grant the wish but with this warning: *Noah would be in the audience.*

In discussing the "terrible truths" of electronic journalism, one finds many "Noahs" out there, quick to compare notes but slow to agree to a set of governing principles. Truthfully, there are no rules for the industry in general, only a motley collection of debatable guidelines. The news department of each television station seems to have its own style and agenda, but between lapses of any *"terrible truths,"* the viewer will, from time to time, have his/her chance to encounter the writing skills of Hemingway, the imagination of Picasso, the photographic excellence of a Hy Peskin or Annie Lebowitz, the courage of a New York Firefighter, the footwork of a flamenco dancer and the balancing act of a flying Wallenda. It does happen but make sure you have a good book to read between those times.

When all is right with the world, a newscast can make for unique, informative and sometimes entertaining and engaging programming. A viewer's response can range from a grateful sense of being well informed, to disgust if he disagrees with the content and how it is presented…or suicidal if his name is mentioned. Agreement among the faithful about principle or presentation is as rare as the late Mother Teresa being whirled around the floor by that flamenco dancer. Formats may be altered from time to time but basic journalism—minus today's electronics and the shameful name-calling in its early years—hasn't changed in a century and a half. The most common admonishment we hear in the profession is to *try to be objective.* Today, being objective in this industry takes stepping over roadblocks of pomposity, stubbornness and ignorance. Again, journalism isn't rumor. Journalism is about verification. Journalism requires facts and the time it takes to check those facts.

My story is one of observation, natural cynicism, personal experience, concern for the profession, love of the media, respect for the history and evolution of journalism…and pride for what can be done when all the pieces fit… and disenchantment when they don't.

As close as I can come to breathing the rarified air of any of today's network anchors and reporters is to remember that my grandfather was best man at Percy Huntley's wedding. Percy became the father of Chet Huntley who is the Godfather to many of today's older TV Anchors. Like Chet, I was born in and spent my formative years in Saco, Montana, located in the Northeast quadrant of the state, described by a 2006 April edition of National Geographic Traveler magazine as being "The Last Real America." Of course, all this didn't so much as a lay a single brick in my yellow brick road of life but did help me appreciate the West and the honestly and integrity that comes from hard working people and wide open spaces. Montana wears its moniker as the "Big Sky" country with pride and honesty.

The Huntleys (Chet's dad and mom) came back to Saco whenever they could…and in her many conversations with my grandmother, Mrs. Huntley always mentioned that Gene should get into TV and "do what Chet is doing." *Do what Chet is doing?* All I needed was an education, a voice, reasonably good looks, an established career, unparalleled ambition, big time connections, a disciplined mind and a pot full of luck.

I didn't lay eyes on a TV set until I was in my mid teens and it would be another decade before a TV newscast would hold any facet of fascination for me. It would take a professor at the University of Montana (Dorothy Johnson —author of *The Man Who Shot Liberty Valance* to encourage me to take a hard look at the opportunities in television, particularly news. However, she said that if I didn't possess a curious and probing mind to forget it and look elsewhere. When I responded by asking where she came up with the name *Liberty Valance*, she smiled and said, "That's not much, but it's a start."

While still a student, a part-time job at the local TV station proved to a valuable experience as well as provide a pivotal episode in the direction I would ultimately take. I was asked to come in and read the noon-time-farm report, a very important piece of news for rural Montana. I wouldn't actually be on camera but in a small announcer booth. A slide with *"Farm Report"* written on it was the only visual. I was no on-air newscaster and didn't have a great desire of even becoming one and to accept this assignment I can only chalk up to pure lunacy and an ego that badly needed an overhaul. I got there just in time to read it, without once having looked at the copy before the mike was turned on. I must admit that even reading a short newscast without preparation is difficult enough for any rational person…but reading a *farm report* cold turkey, with numbers, fractions, canners and cutters and a dozen other unfamiliar terms was unadulterated stupidity. But, reckless with misplaced courage, I plunged into the copy like it was something I did every day of my life. By the third word, however, I knew I was in serious trouble, beginning a fall into an abyss from which there would be no return. The copy made absolutely no sense to me. My throat got drier than an Arizona desert, and in my mind's eye I could envision the farmers out there, who needed the information, assembling a lynch party. I even started to fantasize about how I wanted to kill myself when I finished. It was the longest ten minutes of my life.

It's amazing how a single event can take on a life of its own. Since then I have never done a report or said something in front of an audience unless I was totally prepared. Not that I was ever as smooth as a Matt Lauer but at least I lowered the odds of embarrassing myself. The imprint of those ten minutes of fumbling my way through that bloody farm report lives with me today. I do believe I also made the conscious decision that day of living and working *behind* the camera rather than in front of it.

Amazingly, I did eventually get a full time job at that same station and in due course moved to other larger facilities in the West, most notably KSL Radio and Television in Salt Lake City. It was there I developed enough moxie and dedication to stay and thrive in the same business for a couple of decades as reporter, producer and ultimately as a news director at a rival station. During all that time there was never a moment while reading or being a part of a newscast that I didn't think about that fateful ten minutes early in my life.

There is little that happens in life that doesn't have a corresponding parable. The Bible, preachers, teachers, even comedians regale us with comparisons of two dissimilar looking events but with similar lessons to explain the whys and wherefores of our daily existence. Two seemingly unrelated events can find common ground when trying to illuminate an experience or bring further understanding to the motivation of why people or companies or professions do what they do. For that reason I have included personal stories of incidents in my life that relate, some though remotely, to decisions and principles found in a news room, which, it would seem, to be an appropriate depository of life's experiences, albeit buffeted by the motives, methods and machinery of society.

And, oh yes, I did eventually meet Chet Huntley in New York City after I had been in the business a while. We talked a bit about Montana but more importantly he introduced me to members of the NBC evening news staff that eventually led to an NBC News proposal to be a producer. I didn't take it but was very jacked up about the offer. My grandmother would have been proud.

Questions are the principle tools of journalists. They need to know the answers to the *who, what, why, where, when* and *how* of just about everything they cover. But in between the necessary examination of issues and the needed investigations of industries and personalities dealing with the public trust, there are questions that simply have no answers and issues that never find resolution.

I was once asked the question by a naval instructor when I was 19…

If it took a chicken and a half,
a day and a half,
to lay an egg and a half…
how long would it take a monkey with a wooden leg
to kick the seeds out of a watermelon?

That question, in a variety of forms, he said, will haunt you from time to time and eventually you'll realize you're wasting your time because there is no answer or at least an answer that would provide any comfort to your sense of curiosity.

Impossible or not, good journalists believe there is always an answer, somewhere, trying to make sense of life's absurdities…but also recognize when it is time just to accept an act or event or happening for what it is and move on. The problem viewers face almost nightly is that mediocre journalists will either concoct an answer or confuse them with a profusion of visuals, sound bites and impressions that complicate more then simplify and never fully answer the original question—if there was, indeed, any answer in the first place. Henry Morgan, the late irreverent and irritable broadcaster, once told me that one of the problems with TV newscasts is that the reporters are mostly cowards; if someone says the sun rises in the East, they rush out to find someone who will say it rises in the West. *Courage on the local level is,* he said, *in short supply.*

Still, journalism, in whatever form, is an amazing profession, but it has some idiosyncrasies that baffle more than they benefit, and the viewing public should be more conscious of them. At the same time, the newsroom should *also* be more aware and address them for what they are…and they are…*The Ten Terrible Truths of Local TV News.*

1.

News is a monster,
impossible to totally control
and as changeable in definition as a drifting cloud in an open sky.

2.

If local TV newscasts suddenly ceased to exist,
life, as we know it, wouldn't skip a beat.

3.

You can be absolutely accurate
in the information you present,
and dead wrong in the impression you leave.

4.

Contrary to its own marketing,
a local TV newscast is not the voice of the people
or even an accurate reflection of the community.

5.

You cannot judge a Television news operation by its promotion.

6.

More than journalistic integrity,
spectacular production techniques and wide ranging coverage
---it is the Anchor who carries a station's news image.

7.

Television is a triumph of equipment over people.

8.

Flashing red lights illuminate the stage
of a local TV news operation

9.

An ordinary picture
takes precedence
over the most profoundly written word.

10.

TV News loves to misbehave,
opting for controversy over substance,
image over reality,
and never letting a story die.

1.
News is a monster,
impossible to totally control or define
and as changeable in shape as a drifting cloud in an open sky.

News (nooz,) n.pl.

Information previously unknown—reports, collectively, of recent happenings, esp. those broadcast over radio or TV, printed in a newspaper, etc.—any person or thing thought to merit special attention in such reports

Webster's New World Dictionary

Ah…wouldn't it be wonderful if it were that easy. The definition of *news* is deceptively simple. The trick is to determine what *"recent happening"* or *person or thing* that deserves *special attention* is truly interesting enough to be termed *acceptable* to the viewer or reader. And once *that* has been established, the next step is how to present it to the public, taking into account such debatable considerations as how much time or space to give it, what priority should be given, what production techniques should be used, how much visual to put with it, its value (or lack thereof) to the reader or viewer, what follow-up should be done, etc. Making those decisions separates the committed from the indifferent …and even then, there are pockets of quicksand to swallow even the most dedicated.

I'm not going to name some of my colleagues who are very well known for their television presentation, but they wouldn't know new information or how to report a story if it came up and bit them.

Bob Woodward
Washington Post

Woodward, of all people, knows that part of handling information in the journalism industry is knowing what to do with it once you've got it. It may have a bite to it or it may be so subtle that it flies under the radar. Or it may be that it doesn't have anything to do with anything and is therefore useless in a journalistic setting, whether print or electronic.

Information is information in whatever form it comes to you. And usually, there is some place to put it, though not necessarily on a TV broadcast or in a daily newspaper. There are options out there that will typically take any information about anything. For example, The World News in the tabloid section of the grocery store may talk about the last survivor of the Titanic found alive floating on an iceberg 95 years after the ship sank. Tabloids are known for taking the truth and turning it upside down and inside out, or ignoring it completely. While other pieces of information may be a little more orthodox in content, they may still fall outside of what you would normally find on the evening news.

To accommodate the many varieties of information that come from all directions, the journalism industry has developed, though not consciously or necessarily endorsed, a set of accommodating niches; *straight news, investigative news, advocacy and comment, tabloid news, feature news* and to further confuse the reader/viewer, *soft news* as opposed to *hard news*. In time, we'll discuss each of these types but for purposes of staying within boundaries of understanding, common sense and convenience to the reader, we'll stick mostly to those types more closely linked to reporters, editors and producers in television news…and to a lesser degree, print journalists. On a day to day basis, journalists and their supporting cast deal with these *Terrible Truths* that bring them consternation, confusion, controversy and constipation. Like the viewers, they don't always approve of the way some stories are handled but instinctively know they are balanced by those stories that illuminate issues that affect the lives of all of us.

The first amendment is easy to understand.
It says the government can't tell you how to worship.

It says if you have something to say, you can say it.
If you want to, you can write it down and publish it.
If you want to talk about it with others, you can assemble.
And if you have a grievance,
you can let your government know about it,
and no-one can stop you.

Jim Carey
Scholar, Professor

In his own unique style of cutting through the bull, Carey sums up the essence of the First Amendment in layman's language, saying we have the license to say and print just about anything we want and do it any*where* we want…while at the same time giving reporters journalistic indigestion. For those who have to deal with what people are saying or doing or what they're *going* to do, and then explain it to others, would seem a routine function. But while the First Amendment is being righteously waved, other factors come into play—privacy laws, the sensitivity of the subject, pressure from individuals with vested interests, failure to get adequate or accepted verification, the involvement of a TV station's client, a question of its importance to anyone or anything, and even to the heart, mind and soul of the reporter…all are part of the mix in determining how far to push this First Amendment thing.

Some information crossing a news desk is obvious and objective…but a sizeable, or even an alarming amount, is subjective. Determining what information can be classified as "news" to print or air is a continuing challenge. When asked to define "news" David Brinkley answered, *"News is what I say it is."* This may seem like an incredibly conceited statement but upon reflection it is as close to the *truth* as anyone is going to get when trying to identify what is *news*. (Fifty journalists locked in a room will come up with fifty other definitions, with some truth in all of them.) In the end, when it's time to put a newspaper to bed or a TV station to air the nightly news, the judgment of what gets printed or televised is determined by just a few people or, in most cases, just one man or woman who makes the final decision. In a perfect world, one hopes that one person is experienced, objective, curious, knowledgeable, sensitive, in tune with his community, responsible to his industry and capable of being a proxy for the readers or viewers.

There are going to be those times when a piece of information will be missed or overlooked that would make a significant difference in the story. The changing landscape of defining what news is acceptable will continually color a producer's decisions and thereby influencing those who are on the receiving end. Experience becomes more and more valuable because all that information hurdling at him like a run-a-way freight train can fit into several different journalistic slots. And then, there are times when the information is soooo damn attractive but doesn't mean a thing to anyone…or so titillating in nature, that it surely must be worth an inordinate amount of time and attention.

> *The one function TV news performs very well*
> *is that when there is no news*
> *we give it to you with the same emphasis as if there was…*
> David Brinkley
> NBC/ABC

"Titillating" information is always a strange call to make by a producer of a newscast. For example, one afternoon, the market's top rated TV station, received word that an unmarked box was found sitting in a hallway of a public building. The police bomb squad was summoned to explore its contents, using a detonation device. It was found that the box contained a sewing machine and nothing else. The station led its major newscast with the story, showing the mechanics of what police do in such a situation, interviewing everyone who had something to say…and gave the story roughly three minutes of airtime. Points to repeat: there was a sewing machine in the box, no threatening phone call, no bomb, no-one hurt, no-one arrested, no ongoing investigation, no-one traumatized. Yet it was given three minutes as a lead story on a major newscast…which begs the question, "Was the public served? Was it worth a story other than showing the efficiency of the bomb squad? Of course, the story was valid but only about twenty seconds somewhere in the middle of the newscast. Considering the short period of available time anyway, some stories were probably bumped to make room for this one. Defining what is and is not news is tricky enough without dealing with a story that has no payoff. Granted, a potential bomb is a slam-dunk of a story…but how far do you carry it when there is no bomb, only a possibility. Definition and priorities are ongoing challenges in a newsroom. Giving a story more or less time than it deserves is a daily dilemma.

There are, of course, some stories—in fact quite a few of them—that really don't qualify as hard *or* soft news. Thankfully, they don't pop up often, and when they do there are a myriad of reasons that defy traditional definition and even common sense. Whether a reporter, an anchor or a news director, none are beyond putting in a story to pacify management, cater to a persistent request to cover this or that or just because the video is so good it's hard to not use it. It happens. This business is not rocket science. *Precision, meticulous, perfect, absolute objectivity, flawless, impartial* or *seamless* are not words floating around a newsroom or used to define journalism. So, in the end, it's really not so easy to compare the difference of what is and what is not...*news.* Frankly, the public has a hard time telling the difference anyway.

The public does ask questions, a lot of them, and they are not always about the definition of news, but rather, *where do stations look for news and what criteria is followed when airing it?* On paper there are several main sources of news, among them...

- ...from the inventiveness and curiosity of the reporter,
- ...from the wire services that provides news not only to TV but the newspaper industry as well,
- ...from other members of the media, including other TV stations, radio and the print industry,
- ...from press releases usually provided by public relations firms, special interest groups, and communication departments from different corporations,
- ...from police and fire monitors and eyewitnesses of breaking news,
- ...from follow-up investigations of continuing stories.
- ...from the stories themselves that walk in the front door of the newsroom; the obvious or some thing that was already scheduled on a particular day.

How to determine *what to air* is not an exact science but neither is it decided in a haphazard fashion. Those involved in broadcast news must at least understand the 12 factors that constitute news value, as designed by seasoned journalists...

- *...timeliness.* What's hot today is old news tomorrow.

- *...proximity.* Where it happens is important, the greater the distance the less likelihood it'll see the light of day.

- *...exceptional quality.* How uncommon is the event? Dog biting a man is common. A man biting a dog is uncommon.

- *...possible future impact.* Will the story have legs? Flu strikes. Will there be an epidemic? Sometimes a simple story can lead to the collapse of an institution.

- *...prominence.* A mundane event becomes something more if a celebrity of sorts is involved.

- *...conflict.* Can you spell Iraq or Katrina? Or...the mayor is feuding over something with the governor.

- *...the number of people involved or affected.* The more people involved, the more newsworthy it is.

- *...consequence.* Something happens that has rebounding effects.

- *...human interest.* Soft news with a heart.

- *...pathos.* Stories that evoke a viewer response; tears, anger, compassion.

- *...shock value.* Unique and unexpected happenings.

- *...titillation component.* Sex

One would think that with all these sources and factors of what is newsworthy, there would be a greater variety of stories...but we're sadly learning that people are drawn to the sight of blood and guts above all else, or it could be what the stations like to broadcast. It's easy to find, easy to cover and while it doesn't affect the viewers lives, *there is*, in the words of Frank Lloyd Wright, *enough titillation to make it chewing gum for the eyes.*

Maybe the viewers sometimes get TV programs mixed up with the local news and expect more than a newscast is capable of delivering. But the paradox is that while they seem to like the crime and accident portions of the news, there is also a large segment that *won't watch* for the same reason. But the stations go for the known quantity. Why try to teach a dog a new trick when he seems so happy to keep doing the old one. More on this in the eighth *Terrible Truth*.

One would think that given the same unfolding of events of a single day, each outlet—broadcast or print—would come up with basically the same information, except for feature stories and those that take several days of research. However, on a daily basis, in the conventional media, there is still a wide divergence in what news is covered and what is ignored and how one is the lead story on one station and the tenth story on another, and why a story gets two minutes on one and fifteen seconds by a competitor, or gives the royal treatment to one and is an after-thought by another…and then when the stories on the television stations are compared to what is in the newspapers of the same twenty four hour period, one would swear they were looking at news of another day.

Even on a good day, determining *what is news* is a roll of the dice in the minds of the viewers and readers. They are, for the most part, ready to accept anything put before them. *What* is covered and *how* it is presented is up to the broadcasters and print reporters. On any given day there is a span of topics that is beyond a normal grasp…and when you compare *how* and *what* is covered by four television stations and two major dailies on that particular day, one can see that the selection process of what *is* and *isn't* news will confound even the most experienced.

To say the game is highly competitive is like saying Genghis Khan was a bad neighbor. But every once in a blue moon something will happen that defies the hard-nosed edge of the industry and brings a small level of tolerance and forgiveness by a critical audience. In the spring of 2006, the son of one of the reporters at KTVX in Salt Lake City was killed in a playground accident. On the day of the funeral, the news director of a competing station, KSTU, called the news director of KTVX. More than just voicing his condolences he offered his station's tapes and attending information of the day's happenings so that all the news personnel of KTVX could attend the boy's funeral. It was not just an offer of good will but a bona-fide gift without strings. It was a sad day for the reporter and his family but a proud day for the media. One of the few.

Journalism consists largely in saying Lord James is dead
to people who never knew Lord James was alive.
G. K. Chesterton

The Chesterton quote, in a small way, gently admonishes a reporter that just because he stumbled across pieces of information doesn't mean it all belongs in a newscast. Forty years ago the High Priest of Pop-Culture, Marshall McLuhan wrote that *TV newsmen and women must learn how to handle the information they receive before they turn it loose on the public.* As mentioned, there is hardly a subject or idea that can't find exposure somewhere, considering the media that are available, which only compounds the exercise of defining this monster called *news.* The cloud continues to shift its shape and news continues to evolve.

If you would understand anything,
observe its beginnings and its development
Aristotle

Evolving is what news does best, ever since a Chinese eunuch invented *paper* in the first century. After months of experimentation, Ts' ai Lun presented his Emperor with soaked bamboo sprouts that would change the course of history. While the rest of the world used papyrus, goat and sheep skin, China forged ahead with paper, giving wings to the meaning of the term, *advanced civilization.* For 600 years China was the only nation on earth that knew the secret of papermaking *until* a couple of Chinese paper makers were kidnapped and taken to Persia where the technique was eventually turned loose on the world…with a matching decline in Chinese influence.

In the fourteenth century, Johann Gutenberg put together the essential ingredients of what some say is the most important invention since, ah…*paper* —the printing press. Together, with Ts'ai Lun's soaked bamboo sprouts and now a crank-turning machine of a thousand parts, the two wrought upon the world—**journalism**—the *watchdog of society*. More specifically, it is the reporting of daily events, a commentary on the flow of public activity, the presentation of intentional and unintentional events or actions by man or Mother Nature; the illumination of personal triumphs and tragedies of individuals, groups and countries; the nonsensical wanderings of man in general and despots, dictators and bullies specifically…and the what, why, when, where and how of everything that goes on in society. Initially, the art of the printed word would eventually pique our curiosity, inform us, break our hearts, embarrass us, help us make decisions, give us wisdom, infuriate us, give us nightmares, lift our spirits, enlighten us, create indelible impressions, warn us, begin bar room brawls, reinforce our attitudes or change our minds…and make us think, drool, laugh or gnash our teeth.

God Bless Lun and Gutenberg. We don't know whether to thank or chastise them.   Then, to stir the pot, but not necessarily change people's reaction to the brew, the 20th century introduced us to *electronic* journalism, first radio where a standard of sorts was set for the *presentation* of news…and finally, *television news*, initially radio news with pictures. In the 21st century it has become one of the most dominant forces in society. Never mind that the industry has never had any real guiding set of rules that were cast in stone or firm qualifications to participate. Yet, at first blush, electronic journalism seems absolutely vital to our existence.

The ghosts of Ts'ai Lun and Gutenberg are probably out there somewhere in the cosmos banging their heads against some thunder cloud wondering if their joint creation was really worth this fuss over the transfer of information, whatever the subject matter. And I'm sure they would wonder whether or not the declaration of some human achievement was properly balanced by a tabloid taking someone's life apart…or wondering if the joy of a good book outweighs hate mail or pamphlets advocating the overthrow of governments, religions or individual philosophies.

Ah, there's good news tonight!
Gabriel Heater

You would have to be entering your senior years to know the existence of Gabriel Heater…but in his day he made the news palatable to millions of Americans who were heartsick by the unfolding events of World War II. He always managed to find some piece of news that was positive and uplifting before he spelled out the negatives that only a full-fledged war can bring. But that was then. There are no Gabriel Heaters today but we can thank him for getting radio news off and running for the masses.

By the time radio was introduced, journalism—good & bad—had pretty well been defined by the printed word…but with the sinking of the Titanic, people suddenly caught the importance and drama of the *spoken* word. David Sarnoff, as a 21 year old wireless freak, from the top of a building in downtown New York City, received word that the S.S. Titanic hit an iceberg and was sinking… and for 72 hours relayed information from his wireless unit of the tragedy to those few, *somewhere around a dozen,* who had a receiver. Still, the dawn of electronic journalism was upon us and the sun has yet to set, though it is still— and probably always will be—considered a bastard cousin to the printed word.

And then *television*, if not a *kissin'* cousin to radio, was at least a bully nephew who, when he couldn't follow the rules, made up a list of his own…and is still freelancing and knocking over the furniture. Television newscasts, in one form or another, have been broadcast for over 50 years. On the surface, they now appear to be a fundamental diet of daily life. They can start your morning or end your day in any number of ways, but mainly to let you know what happened that day or night…and whether it's going to literally rain on your parade.

There are, in medium to large sized markets, nearly 25 television daily news-oriented programs—local and network newscasts, interview programs, and evening investigative pieces—are broadcast each morning, afternoon and night on independent, educational and commercial network affiliated stations. Throw in CNN and MSNBC and there are only a few reasons left not to be well informed. Amazingly, there are still stories that fall through the cracks.

The irony of this news blitz is that management of TV stations believes that the viewers actually thrive on the stuff they are fed on the broadcasts and that these same viewers become addicted and cannot function as rational human beings if management doesn't spoon up a healthy dose of TV news several times a day. The network affiliated stations offer a regimen of newscasts to satisfy any schedule, any sex, any age, any interest…and they bet both their bottom dollar *and* bottom line on being successful. But trying to make their viewers dependent on their newscasts is still an iffy proposition. The ratings may sing a different song with too many sour notes. So they try different formulas, but in an effort to be different, they look more and more alike. What is working for one station suddenly becomes the standard and style of another and another. And now with the same basic format, the focus falls on a particular anchor or an emphasis shifting to some other dimension of the news. One station started to use *Breaking News* with some regularity and before long, the term became just as prevalent on the other stations. Granted, the phrase does pique a viewer's curiosity and some sense of excitement, some of which is actually interesting. One local station gives a wink to journalistic ethics and meanings as it promotes itself as one who doesn't just report the news but "takes action to get something changed."

Every station in the market knows that to survive it has to make the viewers— or at least a size able chunk of them—*dependent* on the product they produce. Roughly 40% of the station's income is derived from its newscasts so there is a no-holds barred fight to the finish, each station winning enough viewers to continue the struggle, but always wanting more.

Making a viewer dependent is an ongoing struggle for any station. They might take a lesson from the guy who was challenged to get rid of the boar hogs in the Florida swamplands after decades of hunters, poachers and trappers trying every scheme under the Florida sun to get rid of the damn things. But the hogs were so used to surviving on roots, bugs and other unappetizing delights that they cancelled out every effort to clear them out. So one day a man with an axe and a bag of oats came tromping into the swamp. He found a reasonably solid piece of ground and proceeded to cut away a clearing. As he worked, he daily poured a pile of oats in the middle of the clearing, quickly getting the attention of the hogs. Little by little the baby hogs would run in, grab a mouth full and run out…but they got braver when they realized the man just ignored them, going on about his work. Finally, the adult hogs didn't want to lose out so they too would come in to get their share.

It became a daily routine for both the man and the hogs. What the hogs didn't notice was that the man was putting up a fence around the clearing and one day when all the hogs were pigging out, the man dropped in a gate, closing off any chance for escape.

A truck was brought in and the hogs were hauled away. When asked how he did it…the man said, *"I can trap anything or anyone that I can make dependent on me."* And therein lies the formula for a TV station anxious to build an audience. Give the people a daily dose of oats disguised as terrific graphics, a pleasing anchor, snappy promotion, hip headlines and maybe, just maybe, they will become *dependent* on the station's newscasts. With all that money flowing in, management may be able to buy enough oats to feed the news department with even more imagination, desire and commitment to meet the sacred responsibility to inform people about stories to which they can relate and use to help chart and influence parts of their own lives. At least that's how the fantasy should play out. (Jimmy Hoffa has a better chance at making a surprise appearance at the next AFL-CIO meeting)

Making people dependent on their product is always a worthy goal for any business and TV stations do all they can to reinforce that concept, most of which means doing the same old stuff, but more of it…and listening to consultants who think they have all the answers to Jeopardy and, more important, what they think viewers want. They follow the old P.T. Barnum philosophy of *never underestimating the taste of the American public* so it's no accident that flashing red lights dictate the direction a nightly newscast will take…and that nearly 50% of that newscast will be composed of crime and accidents. Not surprisingly, the other stations do the same things, though most of what they do and how they do it is predicated on how much money they have to spend. The big dogs with a pot full of it don't easily share their bones and are out to squash the competition…which is the way the game is played in every market.

Journalists are like dogs,
whenever anything moves, they begin to bark.
Arthur Schopenhauer

And they have been barking for a long time. One who took serious note and listened carefully to the *what*, *where*, *why* and *when* of the barking was Walter Cronkite, "The Most Trusted Man in America." The people may have seen him as Father Walter, but to the journalist, he was considered purely as *a hard news man*. He wasn't nuts about feature stories or other fluff because it took away from the business at hand; namely, the hard stuff describing *what* was happening, *how* it happened and *what* it meant to the people. He wasn't beyond expressing his own opinion—and did, on air—but he lamented that *news was being compressed into tiny tablets and everyone was to take a pill of news every day...and that,* he said, *was suppose to be enough.* He recognized that the dogs never shut up. And now with Twitter, Facebook and YouTube, I can only imagine how Walter would react...and is probably glad he doesn't have to deal with it. He had already made his considerable contribution.

Today, exposure to television news is like back pain; it never seems to go away. To some viewers, that newscast is critical to their desire to be well informed, but they are in the minority. There is a downside. Actress Sarah Bernhard—(I never, ever thought that in my lifetime that I'd be quoting Sarah Bernhard)—said, *when watching the news, how many days in a row can you watch and still feel good about yourself and the world.* Begrudgingly, she has a point, a very good one. Somewhere on some station—morning, noon and night—there seems to be a newscast to enlighten, inform, or illuminate something. Some of it might even be interesting. It may be too much for some but not to others. They like the thought of some reality of the world and some of the local events to flood into a viewer's living room. More than the printed word, television will give us a stronger visceral experience of what has happened during the day. It will put a face to a voice and save you a trip to see the car that ran into someone's living room. And like the reader of the printed word, a viewer can, on occasion, experience a wide range of emotions—anger, concern, depression, exhilaration and, most important, the satisfaction of being informed about a changing world. Television news tries to do it all, and, graphically, it's getting better all the time...but the medium and the message are too often estranged.

The flow of information is not a gentle, lazy stream drifting in and out of a viewer's home. It is buffeted by several undercurrents that can rock a sturdy boat. Video tape has to be shot and edited, copy has to be written, graphics have to be constructed, live reports have to be produced, the anchorman has to set up the story …and in a flawless world, everything falls perfectly into place. But to make it happen takes time, intelligence, focus, commitment and a clear head. When all the pieces have to be forced, which is most of the time, you have a public on your back, management in your face and public officials at your throat. To some journalists, this is called heaven on earth. To others, it means they are just doing their job. And even beyond the serious news, there is nothing wrong with those lighthearted moments that remind us not to take ourselves so seriously.

You throw the ball. You hit the ball.
You catch the ball. You got that?
The movie: Bull Durham with baseball manager explaining the basics.

Like baseball and other professions, electronic journalism has its basics. You find the story. You cover the story. You present the story. But like baseball, there are variations and degrees of difficulty that complicate, confuse and challenge those who want to participate. Thankfully, those who don't like or can't handle the bare bones of the business with some expertise don't last. And like baseball, the public makes the final judgment.

For the most part, the public has been amazingly tolerant but still gets cranky and tells the folks of electronic journalism to get their act together and give the people a real reason to watch as well as listen. We have to accept the fact that print journalists are better in some areas but at the very least, electronic journalists are an alternative to those who want the news and don't have a lot of time, remembering we are caught up in this *no-read* society. Still, we have to recognize that while television news has extended the borders of its business, it too often falls short in trying to control the ebb and flow of its work on a daily basis. Electronic journalism can be a delicate flower of compassion or a steamroller of conviction. As a viewer you can take it on but you'll feel like the proverbial one-legged man in a butt-kicking contest. Without a TV camera and access to the media your odds of winning are considerably reduced. A few have won a battle but some have suffered a humiliation that can extend beyond the grave. We'll talk about it.

The conflict between the men who make the news
and the men who report the news is as old as time.
News may be true, but it is not truth,
and reporters and officials seldom see it the same way.
In the old days, the reporters or couriers of bad news
were often put to the gallows;
now they are given the Pulitzer Prize or an Emmy
...but the conflict still goes on.

James Reston
Columnist

The conflict between newsmakers and news reporters is, like Army-Navy football, one of life's eternal struggles. And while appreciating the journalist's contribution to our bank of knowledge, there are still a size able number of congressmen, corporations and celebrities that favor the gallows as a way of dealing with reporters who broadcast bad news. Emmys and Pulitzers aside, journalists thrive on trouble and threats and daily knock twice on their seemingly impenetrable shield of protection by the First Amendment.

After having produced a couple thousand television newscasts and being a part of the conspiracy to convince people that our news is making some kind of contribution in their lives, I find myself in turmoil trying to put some kind of definition to what it is that I did and others are still trying to do. At conception, it would appear that the late local newscasts, with the biggest audience of the day for news, would not only be informed but enlightened. It should give us something of substance on which to grab and hope it gives us some understanding as to what is going on in our world or even our neighborhood. Most of it however, really doesn't do anything for the people except to scantily fill them in on what has happened during the day. It only infrequently relates to their lives in some way.

There isn't enough news in the half hour period with news, weather, sports and commercials thrown in to really examine any issue with the clarity it deserves. Again, about 50 percent of the news is crime (shootings, robberies, etc.) and accidents—which most newspapers don't even mention or are relegated to the back pages. Sadly, there is only about 5 minutes that is available for news that has some lasting effects on the lives of the viewers. David Brinkley said that… *most of the news isn't very important. In fact, very little of it is.* Most nights on the news, local reporters and producers are trying very hard to prove Brinkley's point.

2.
If local TV news suddenly ceased to exist,
life would hardly skip a beat.

.

Billy Crystal: *Hi Curly, kill anyone today?*
Jack Palance: *The day ain't over yet!*

The movie, City Slickers

Sadly, too many people see television news journalists as vultures waiting for the worst in mankind to show itself on any given day. A killing, however it is done, represents meat and potatoes to a television newsroom. It's visual, it's noisy and it has a great cast of characters. And television does it better than any other medium. Yet, unless it happens in your home or on your doorstep, it rarely affects anyone of us. We watch it, nod or shake our heads, make a comment about how terrible or sad or tragic it is, then we quickly move on and forget the basics of the event half way through the next story in the newscast.

Promotion, marketing, beautiful people, and ratings to the contrary you simply don't need to watch the current crop of local newscasts. Without them you can still be a productive, well-informed, creative, successful individual. You still have radio, newspapers, *network* newscasts, magazines, the art of conversation, and some parts of the Internet. If you are really hard up, there is also face book, twitter and sex chat rooms, but they produce all that is dreary, dribbling, dull and dangerous. Of course, you won't convince the occupants of local television newsrooms of the fact they are not needed by their viewers…and neither should you try. In their favor, reporters, producers, photographers, assignment editors, graphic artists and anchors help allow you, in the words of the late anchorman John Chancellor, *to feel the "fur" of what goes on in the world.* For many, 'the fur' is not warm and fuzzy to the touch; it's more like rubbing against the prickly hair on the back of a crazed badger. Unfortunately, more and more people prefer to feel the "fur" of a *Seinfeld* or *Everyone Loves Raymond* reruns instead of wondering what is going on in the world or what new medical breakthrough is on the horizon, unless, as I have said, it is *breaking news* in which the viewer has a personal interest or natural curiosity. But it goes much further, thankfully.

*I can't imagine anything more
dangerous than a society in which the
news industry has more or less collapsed*

Rosa Brooks
Professor, Law Center
Georgetown University—April 2009

Ms. Brooks expresses an attitude that is becoming all too real in the nation. Her viewpoint is both shared and reinforced by Karl Idsvoog, professor at Kent State University and former investigative reporter. He has been saying for years that, *"When journalism fails, bad things happen!"* One only has to look at Iraq, Enron, the U.S. financial meltdown and a calamitous oil spill to observe the suffering of what happens when journalism fails. *A journalist's job is to verify, not endorse some rumor,* and because this simple definition was lost in Iraq, there was a price to pay in terms of soldiers, time, money and credibility. Failing to ask questions and turning a blind eye to red flags waving like crazy over troubled businesses like Enron and other financial institutions that approved *liar* loans—knowing they would fail—was catastrophic for the while country. Journalists also ignored the antiquated emergency response plan of an offshore oilrig. The terrible truth of all these examples is that journalism failed and bad things happened. Journalists forgot about journalism and instead became cheerleaders, usurping the suspected talents of advertising and public relations people.

Journalism, whether print or electronic, in this era of downsizing and uncertainty, still has a breath or two left to report and examine, but has to do it with fewer people and limited resources. Granted, in 2008 and 2010, collapse became a hard reality for corporations, industries of all type and financial institutions—from the bank on the corner to a Wall Street brokerage firm. And almost all businesses started cutting back in personnel and thinking outside the box—mainly because the box was gone. Local stations were hit particularly hard.

The hard reality in some areas is that the ranks of journalism are continuing to dwindle and are left with nothing but—as columnist Rosa Brooks describes it—*the yapping heads who dominate cable "news" and talk radio; how will we recognize, or hope to forestall, impending national and global crises? How will we know if government officials have made terrible mistakes, as even the best will sometimes do? How will we know if government officials have told us terrible lies, as the worst have sometimes done? A decimated, demoralized and under-resourced press corps hardly questioned President George W. Bush's administration's flimsy case for war in Iraq—and the price for failure will be paid for generations.*

Politics aside, Ms. Brooks makes a strong case for having a robust journalism industry and also has indicated that the slide began years ago. Television news is feeling the same crunch as the newspaper industry. Layoffs are seen and felt in markets of all sizes. Money, we are constantly told, is just not available and resources, patience, and sanity are in short supply.

Not only are experienced journalists being released but other measures are waiting at the gate: having one anchor per newscast, sharing helicopters and reporters with other stations to cover mundane events, concentrating on local news that is quick and easy to cover and present to the public, such as accidents and crime, all to the loss of knowledge and reasons to watch a particular channel. Rating system gurus will collectively have a cardiac arrest trying to figure this one out.

As mentioned, viewership is down over the past decade. So-called *brain dead viewers* seem to survive very handily in the world. Some have even jumped-started their cerebral potentials and are rediscovering the joys of reading and the upscale programming on PBS, A&E, The Discovery Channel and the History Channel. Come to think of it…not many are doing that either.

When I first started in the industry, it was my opinion that everyone out there in TV land faithfully embraced the local news product and that they couldn't function rationally without it that they hung on every word like it was a gift handled down from the News Gods. Over time I realized two opposing and confusing points of view. Viewers are more intelligent than we give them credit for and yet, how gullible they can be. This paradox has proven to be at the foundation of much of the frustration experienced by critics, correspondents and viewers alike. It is a contradiction that makes any analytical statement(s) about news doubly difficult to accept and totally understand.

The original undeclared premise of a newscast on television has been to report the bare bones of the news of the day— *what* happened, *how* it happened, *when* it happened, *where* it happened, *who* did it and *who* did it affect…and it would all be read by the anchorman with whatever visual the station could scare up, from photos to time-worn film. But the evolution of news became more like Henry Ford's, Model T. Eventually, buyers were given the color of their choice, a convertible option, five-on-the-floor or an automatic shift. Predictably, the buyer would even be able to buy the car that more comfortably fits his or her personality.

Similarly, the news went from one anchor—a John Cameron Swayze—reading the vital statistics of a story live on-camera or with dated film, to the addition of specific film and videotape. Interviews, commentary, investigative reporting and graphics were eventually added, among others. With multi- stations broadcasting the same news the viewers could then select the anchorperson of their choice.

As the auto industry kept coming up with new wrinkles, so too did electronic journalism. Off the wall graphics, satellite feeds from anywhere in the world and breaking news reported minutes after it happens, have all become standard…and heaven help us what to expect in the future. We could probably still just get along today with both the Model T *and* a John Cameron Swayze, but it wouldn't be nearly as much fun and certainly our visual knowledge would be limited…but we would survive. Over time one *has* fared better than the other. The Model T is spoken of in reverent tones while Mr. Swayze is remembered more for mixing commercials with the news. Who can forget, *Timex takes a lickin' but keeps on tickin'.*

Hey boy, I say boy...you're doing a lot of choppin'
but no chips are flying
Foghorn Leghorn

Considering what is going on in the world today...and all the talk that is being dispensed, one would think people would be more informed, more involved and smarter...however, experts feel that today's viewers, watching the local news, aren't being informed now anymore than when Swayze was reading the news *with dated film.* Today, flashing red lights seem to get in the way of seeing anything beyond that which doesn't affect us personally and doesn't really expose nearly what it should to complete our daily education of the community and our relationship to it. In later truths we'll examine this slippery slope of transferring information, a subject, frankly, we may be taking too seriously.

Transportation—whether in a Model T or a Ferrari, walking on foot or driving a semi—is still just getting from point A to point B...and *information* is still data passed from one person to another, whether whispering in someone's ear, listening to the radio, typing on an Internet link to a newspaper, actually reading a store bought paper, talking to someone by satellite on the other side of the globe, or watching television. Of course, the way something is transferred—whether it's inventory *or* information—is what affects every single person on earth and is at the center of society's gravitational force. And *transportation* and *information* will dictate most of the continuing changes in the world. Almost everything relates to one or the other. For both to reach their full potential takes superb mechanics, progressive thinking, gobs of money, creative minds that are off the scale and unselfish contributors. In the meantime, both the *transportation* and *information* channels will be clogged with people who serve the wrong masters, who worship idols of green & gold and cater to the selfish and anxiety sides of our nature. I guess they are here to bring balance to all this wonderful progress. I prefer W.H. Auden thoughts on the matter; we *are here on earth to do good to others. What the others are here for, I don't know. "*

One of our both triumphs and tragedies is television news;
We have the freedom but not the courage.

Albanian novelist
Skender Drini

Freedom and courage were rare commodities during the fifty years Albania was under the communist thumb and even now, one is still lacking.

Watching the news for most viewers in the U.S. is a routine, but *if* there is something else going on, watching the local news has a low priority. While serving in Albania on a Knight Fellowship I learned that the vast majority of the population waited anxiously for their local news each night. Everything else, and I mean *everything else*, in their lives is scheduled around the news hour. Next to Spanish soap operas (go figure), the news programs were far and away the most watched programs of the day. The main reason is they do not have the alternative news sources and distribution means of countries like the USA. They take their news very seriously and viewers generally believe what is reported. The problem is that *what was reported was generally biased, inaccurate or poorly presented.* If nothing else, the presentation in the U.S. is a nightly Ziegfeld Follies production and the information is scrutinized ad nauseam. But compared to the committed, passionate viewers in Albania…our news, even with all its bells and whistles, does not hold the viewers full attention and call to action.

One Albanian reporter told me that the citizens in his country want it straight, without flare and commentary. They, frankly, just want to have the information spoon fed to them. A problem and one of the reasons I was there was to encourage the stations to be leery of some of the news content because Albanian legislators would pick out a reporter of some station and get him/her to report his agenda, a practice done with increasing frequency. To further compound the problem was that the viewers generally accept the news as truth-on-a-platter, rarely questioning any of the content. This attitude in the U.S. would be utopia for the media. Thankfully, there are enough critics and selective viewers out there who hold up a cross during every newscast. Still, it is amazing just how much power the U.S. media have and is continuing to build. But of course, progress and change also bring along the stumbling blocks of arrogance, presumption and inaccuracy.

While no one is hoping for a revival of John Cameron Swayze, there is grave concern over the power and free hand given the media. In the 21st Century, it is inconceivable that Swayze would do his own commercials during a newscast. It would certainly not be against any law today for an anchor to do such a thing but it would only happen over the dead bodies of the news director and every reporter in the newsroom. But if we let our minds wander a little we have to admit that the…*takes a lickin' and keeps on tickin'* slogan is not a bad line to illustrate many of today's concerns.

There are so many issues that directly affect us in one way or another, yet the media fails to turn them over and examine the crawly little bugs underneath that are comfortable in their environment and feeling protected when, in truth, they should be exposed and swept away. But that's asking the media to work a little harder, be a little smarter, have more courage, remember why they are in the profession in the first place and be a beacon to that viewer who needs every advantage to protect his family on a dozen different levels as well as just surviving day to day. And that beacon should not be a flashing red light but a steady light shone on those areas of the community that could use something or someone to help sharpen the focus on what should and shouldn't be done.

Journalism: …an ability to meet the challenge of filling time and space.
Rebecca West

There is the one disturbing fact that is dragged out of the dust bin during every journalistic argument about the value of receiving news on the TV vs. the newspaper; *all the words in an entire television newscast would fill only a portion of page one of the newspaper,* hardly enough to call oneself well informed. Filling the *space* available to the print media and filling the *time allotted* to television is a no-brainer. Heaven and hell only know there is enough going on to fill both. As mentioned in first *Terrible Truth*, the real challenge is the selection process, particularly for television. The choices may seem obvious to producers, being conditioned as they are to whatever is easiest to cover, namely petty crime and something crashing into something else. But there is still that overriding sense of pride held by a few journalists who seek out the items to which viewers can relate and will have an impact on their lives. Some stations and reporters do it amazingly well. Even at that, there are the influencing factors of the remaining *Terrible Truths* that erode even the best intentions of the most dedicated professionals.

Television news operations have a real problem;
they don't have a page two.

Art Buchwald

In the 21st Century, local news in the newspaper and local broadcast news have taken diverse paths. News is still news but video dominates and dictates. Flashing red lights blind us to competent, descriptive copy that flesh out more detail. The phrase, *a picture is worth a thousand words,* is reinforced in the opening of nearly every TV newscast in the country, stories that barely see the light of day in the local section of the newspaper.

There are two statistics that broadcasting and print operations are in agreement. *Viewership*, after a slide, is leveling off in the first decade of the 21st century and *readership* is definitely down. In fact, newspaper publishing across the country is in a quick sand of apathy.   Some surveys indicate that 70% of the people get their news from television. This claim is challenged by various researchers…but whether it's 70% or 50% or even 30%, it's a disturbing admission even among committed electronic journalists who, contrary to popular belief, do appreciate a well-informed public.

Ironically, the print media is experimenting with *electronics* for greater distribution of its product. Whatever the stats are with reader and viewership, there is nothing like a Sunday morning with a cup of something and the newspaper. They go together like peanut butter and jelly. It is one of life's simple pleasures that, hopefully, will never go away.

The Internet has become a major player in the dissemination of news and caters to young, busy readers and viewers enhanced even more by the iPad and other electronic "devices." The problem with news on the Internet is that the viewer/reader chooses what they want to see and read. Much like the newspaper they read and watch on TV that truly interests them…and this generally includes a lot of what is already on TV—the spectacular, the violence, the accidents, the nutty stuff, the unique and strange. What they don't get on the Internet is generally the news that can make a difference in their lives—medical breakthroughs, new laws, newly available services, people who are challenging old practices, the revelations of what are needed in the community, among others.

The FCC is trying to be positive with the Internet when it says…
If all goes well, the Internet will one day open wide avenues to enhance the in-depth journalism the country needs. If all goes well, we will find platforms where diverse voices don't just talk, but where they actually have a shot at being heard. There is a lot of commendable experimentation going on to devise innovative models for Internet journalism. I hope these experiments propagate and multiply. As of June 15, 2011, however, what we have gained in support for news and journalism on the Internet does not match what we have lost in the traditional practice of those crafts. <u>Simply put, the Internet cannot fulfill its democratic potential without sustainable journalism.</u>

Most local news operations have their own web sites and the content of their news can be read along with connecting video, but it's also after-the-fact. Live local news *is* actually offered all day long. Of course, whenever the news *is* being broadcast, the constant hope is that stories of influence and impact will be presented. Unfortunately, some of these stories are broadcast at a time in the afternoon when the viewership is down, way down. Those twenty five daily news programs in a medium size market, as well as Oprah and Dr. Phil and their ilk, contain a great deal of useful information, that is, if the viewer doesn't get tired and start watching sitcom reruns. Unfortunately, most of the day-time news programs go wanting for an audience. And those people who really need the information are busy making a living. In actual fact, it is the evening newscasts, particularly the late news, that has by far the biggest audience

> *TV news can only present the bare bones of a story;*
> *it takes a newspaper, with its*
> *capability to present vast amounts of information*
> *to render the story truly boring.*
> Dave Barry

Barry, an accomplished humorist, is probably right on the money when addressing the younger generation. Readership *is* down and falling but still you have to give the *print* media its due. I don't know who said it but you have to admit that … *newspapers are a rough draft of history,* boring or not. Let's hope that history doesn't have to wait until archeologists retrieve unread dusty newspaper print from the archives which will flesh out the cliff notes version of history we get from videotapes or discs or whatever format will evolve over the next one hundred years.

As expected, TV station management and sales managers love to rub that 70% viewership figure in the face of any potential client who would listen. Journalistic integrity seems to be lost on a salesperson anxious to make a buck. It's no secret that anyone from sales is as welcome in a newsroom as a snake in a bird's nest. When a salesman walks into a newsroom, the news staff knows that he/she is up to no good. If he isn't trying to get someone to cover some non-news thing their client was doing or about to do, he is trying to clean up his client's messes.

At times, there are real stories about businesses that give a gut-check to their advertising and sales representatives. A case in point deals with a popular dairy in Utah that was substantially fined by the federal government for violating a hard and fast law about pricing. Not surprisingly, radio, TV and newspapers jumped on it with a vengeance. A major dairy with its finger on the scale was fresh meat for a hungry media. In fact, it was our lead story on our Six p.m. newscast. As it turned out, the dairy just happened to spend big bucks at our station on a daily basis. A TV salesman would have sold his brother-in-law to keep the story off the air but most knew it was futile to even suggest it. But there are those brave souls who will venture forth. When the newscast was over I received a visitor from the advertising agency representing the dairy. He was a senior vice president and a highly respected and powerful member of his industry. On any given day he could scare the pants off any one of our TV salesmen. When he spoke, everyone listened. When he was upset, dishes crashed to the floor. I knew the man well and gave an appropriate greeting. He asked to step into a vacant office where he proceeded to recite chapter and verse about how much money over the years his agency had channeled to our station with this particular account, and that *"it might be appropriate to cut the dairy a little slack over this silly mistake."* I told him that the fine was in place, that it had not been challenged by the dairy, that it affected everyone who purchased the dairy's products, that we had talked with government officials about specifics of the action taken, that we had offered officers of the company a chance to comment but they declined the invitation to go on camera. In my best voice of indignation, I asked *why*, instead of taking us to task, didn't he march into the dairy offices and dress them down for putting him in such a delicate position of defending their indefensible action. *"Silly"* was hardly the word to use. He looked me straight in the eye and said, *"You just don't get it."* …and walked out.

We led with the story again on the late news. To this day I don't know what he meant by *"not getting it."* The one thing I *did* get was that the newspapers and TV stations had a field day with the story...and the dairy closed its doors a year later. Did this stop salespersons from trying to protect a client on the brink, or wanting to promote a non-news story of a new store opening? Did Mother Teresa ever play center field for the New York Yankees?

Management greed is a boil on the backside of any newsroom. While there is pressure to air some stories to soothe the wrinkled brow of a client, there are also stories that are simply untouchable and the thought of airing them would burst a major blood vessel of any TV salesman. Two industries in particular that continue to raise the ire and interest of the viewer with their persistent and, at times, insufferable commercials are the payday loan businesses with their exorbitantly high interest rates...and second, those attorneys who, in 30 and 60 second commercials, show how they are sticking it to insurance companies to the tune of hundreds of thousands of dollars a pop. Even a glance of a reporter's eye toward either industry for the purpose of doing an investigative report would stop the world in mid rotation. Taking away money that could always be faithfully counted upon, as the Roadrunner out- foxing Wile E. Coyote is something that management, stockholders, investors and Boards of Directors just don't appreciate, particularly when a news department decides its time to use a little courage and act independently.

In fairness, the industries discussed are working within the boundaries of the law but they are so unbelievable in their claims that a sizeable chunk of potential viewers are more than a little curious about how these businesses operate and how they manage to pull it off. To these members of commerce, any hint of criticism or examination is tantamount to pouring sand in the gears of a TV station's operating machinery. The simple fact that loan companies in particular are gouging their clients with huge interest rates and are being banned in some states for taking advantage of desperate people, does not seem to enter into a station's sense of ethics when deciding to happily accept their advertising dollars. The mere thought of a reporter even saying the word, *investigation,* is sacrilege to management. *You don't*, as management has said since the beginning of time, *bite the hand that feeds you.*

What passes for investigative journalism is finding someone
with their pants down—literally or otherwise.
                                             Robert Scheer.

Well, that's what most people think investigative journalism is all about…and sometimes it is, but only rarely. Most local investigative reporting generally deals with some issue that does indeed affect the viewer in some fashion. The downside is that investigative stories are rare and usually air only during the rating periods, preceded by enough promotion to remind every one who has ever looked at a television set of what was coming their way.

Generally, investigative reporting has no time frame for airing. Sometimes it's predicated on being able to partner up with stories of similar interest. There is, of sorts, a competition with other stories to be aired at all. Some may stay in the "can" for several days or weeks before there appears to be an appropriate time for their debut, and then it is dependant on how good or sensational or pertinent they are to the moment at hand. Even then, there is always the potential of a lawsuit if the investigation is flawed at some point along the way. If an investigation is thorough, as it should be, it still has the cross to bear of trying to be succinct in content and delivery. There are only a few minutes available for anything in depth unless the entire newscast is dedicated to the story and there is no chance of that happening. In ½ hour there are weather, sports, the cheesy petty crime and accident stories and commercials that are standing in line waiting to be aired. As alluring as it might be to *'find someone with their pants down'*—to speak fugitively—there are still only a few minutes available to air all the grubby details. There was time when a half hour documentary would be produced to do an investigative piece with style and credibility, but locally produced documentaries have gone the way of the Dodo Bird. These days management isn't going to take the chance of losing a few rating points during prime time. No-sir-ree-bob.

It's hard to be an equal partner in the Fourth Estate if you're only keeping the lawn mowed in front of the house and your shoes are only being shined on the toes. Technology (the 7th *Terrible Truth*) is trying to help. A development called a *teletext crawl* now allows a viewer to receive more and more information on the television screen. But there is somewhat of a drawback. The viewer has to master the art of splitting his attention enough to *listen* to an anchor reading a story about an intoxicated man breaking into a museum and *smearing* paint over dozens of artistic renderings and at the same time *read* the crawl at the bottom of the screen announcing that a Hollywood actress celebrated her 33rd birthday with a destructive wild party with her artist husband who was well oiled. In retelling what the viewer saw and heard…it might come out as the actress *painted 33 pictures and celebrated in a museum where her husband drank a fifth of Smirinof's*.

.

Caution to a young reporter:
Be wary. If your mother says she loves you, check on it.
Ed Eulenberg

Credibility is the one quality both the journalist and the viewer/reader cannot live without. If someone says something, journalists must verify and verify again. Considering the viewers insistence on television being their major source of news, it should also be very important to them.

The problem is that most take what they see and hear at face value. William Safire and his brother Leonard Safir (T*hey have elected to spell their names differently*) quote Harland W. Warner on how viewers, readers or listeners should act when checking news. He admonishes… *to mix their mediums. Compare the accounts. Read, listen and view the news every day. Read critically. Seek out opposing views. Don't be headline happy. Read and listen intently. Watch for qualifying words and source limitations. Don't accept charge as conviction, rumor as fact or reliable source as authority.*

Ah, wouldn't it be nice if viewers did just that. Only in our dreams! In the meantime TV news scoops up that couch potato mentality and talks to it, makes love to it, makes no apology, takes no prisoners and takes home a bundle and all the while, to quote Marianne Means of the Hearst Newspaper group, …*allows trivial distractions to dominate television, with celebrity gossip given more air time than serious investigations.*

Over the years, television reporters have come a long way in trying to be an indispensable cog in the journalistic profession. As mentioned in the *First Terrible Truth*, but bears mentioning again, in addition to the time and space factors, producers and reporters have to deal with the realization of the *different kinds of journalism*. Each has a laughable set of written standards and each flies in the face of the other. The many prisms they look through for resolution bring different answers, different styles, different excuses, different attitudes and different prejudices. Fortunately, or unfortunately, each seems to have found a home.

> *You guys wanted to hurt me bad. You wanted me to jump off the bridge. I finally have jumped. You wanted to bring me down.*
> *You finally have brought me and my family down.*
> *So now go pick a different person. I'm done.*
> Barry Bonds

Bonds was referring to investigative reporting and echoed what many others have been saying about Bonds for decades, but the truth is high profile individuals have been media targets since Horace Greeley was burped as a baby. Unfortunately, a celebrity in whatever sport or industry—and especially the men and women who fascinate the public with their slight of hand in business—are fair game for aggressive reporters. What a "hanging judge" in the Old West was to cattle thieves, what Bobby Fischer was to checkmate, what Bobby Knight was to a referee…Mike Wallace was to a news interview. No one could ask the tough question more efficiently or effortlessly than Mr. Wallace. There's an old saying that says… *you know you're going to have a bad day if Mike Wallace is in your office waiting to talk with you.* Wallace may have had the national reputation but there are enough local boys and girls out there who love to pin some poor sap up against the wall. These qualities can be interpreted as having the *killer instinct.*

I once worked with a reporter, Karl Idsvoog, who had exposed a fraudulent alternative medical practice. He had the treasured *killer instinct*, which may have had something to do with his own initials. When one of our other reporters encountered the doctor behind the practice, he asked how he felt about Karl. The doctor said… *ask a fire hydrant how it feels about dogs*. Score one for the doctor…but Karl still eventually uncovered all the facts and I think the good doctor is now selling aluminum siding in Southern Utah.

When it comes to leveling an individual, I generally didn't have the stomach to reach too far into their personal life. It's one thing to spell out his professional troubles or inefficiencies or crimes thereof…but to lift up the blanket to see his private transgressions, moral lapses or stumbling—intentional or not—is not my cup of tea. Admittedly, there are those times when it is necessary to fetter out the facts and explain how those details affect citizens of the community. In all investigative reporting it should never be personal though you'll never convince the subject of an investigation.

During a particularly slow news afternoon I was snooping around the city's ancient City & County Building that has more nooks and crannies then most medieval European castles. I happened to turn a corner where some office furniture was being stored and on top of one of the dusty desks was a prominent city official getting very cozy with a secretary. I muttered some apology and quickly left. Later at the station I received a call from the official who asked if we could talk. I said that might be a good idea and drove back to the City-County Bldg. Of course, he was nervous and asked what my intentions might be. I told him I saw nothing, would repeat nothing to anyone and for him to get on with his life and live up to his reputation as a faithful family man. He was relieved and though I asked him for nothing I was amazed how cordial and accommodating he was to me for the next few years. What he had done meant nothing to me or to our viewers, unless, of course his dalliance somehow interfered with his work or affected the taxpayers. It was not for me to judge though I know some 'journalists' would salivate finding a way to connect the dots. I'm convinced this so-called *killer instinct* is not a natural trait. It is an aberration of human behavior. I don't think you are born with it but some acquire it through their environment and experiences in life and some, working in the journalism profession, have it thrust upon them in the name of survival.

I am always apologizing for it,
criticizing it, defending it, praising it, damning it, loving it, and hating it,
…that glamorous enfant terrible of journalism, television news
Don Breshahan.

...so says every politician at one time or another. There is always something that will set someone off on any given newscast. It is an occupational hazard for anyone in the industry. Being loved by everyone all the time is, regrettably, unrealistic Journalists and producers will consistently—and will probably always continue to do so—wound someone in the community who

made the Late News on something that was, if not illegal, at least awkward or humiliating in some fashion. Their attitude, which may conflict with a viewer's opinion, has always been that it is not the reporter's fault. It is a *terrible truth* about the profession but, as stated earlier, it is one they have learned to live with, albeit not comfortably. They just report the points of interest surrounding the story. If it happens to be shameful, degrading, embarrassing, crushing or mortifying...so be it. That's how the game is played on both sides.

Seeing suffering, and worse, *causing* suffering are part and parcel of journalism. It is an accepted traditional practice to spell out every negative in someone's high profile life and use everything possible to hype the story in some manner, even if what they did was not illegal or harmful to anyone. The mere act of having been charged with something is generally reason enough to look under every shiny stone in someone's life, guilty or not. Many subjects of these investigations never fully recover, but there are those with an inner strength that defies anything that can be done to them.

When I was about fifteen I once shot a rock into a flock of seagulls and scored a direct hit on one that fell with a sickening thud to the ground, seemingly dead to the world. But in a few minutes the wing of the gull fluttered a little and step-by-step there was a rebirth. He managed to stand upright and I could see where the rock hit, smack in the middle of the left eye. After ten minutes or so it took off...right into the side of our outside garage. Another knockout. From a short distance away I watched the process of recovery repeat itself. And again the bird took off. But this time, straight and away. I never saw it again but I'll never forget what happened. I think the killer instinct died in me that day. So what ultimately happened? I moved to a state that had made the seagull the state bird and is protected by state law. Amazing! Lawmakers aren't so lucky.

Like the seagull, a wounded politician or official will spend a while recuperating and then venture out into the public arena again only to suffer the expected stares and comments…but eventually, if his or her constitution is strong enough, they'll take flight again and get on with their life. Still, whatever happens down the line, there will always be that wound that never heals and the ache that never goes away.

A reporter will look for any wrinkle to increase interest in a story, even if means getting personal. The press—print and electronic—loved to refer to Scott Peterson, who was convicted of murdering his pregnant wife in a sensational 2004 trial, as a "fertilizer salesman" throughout his trial, as if nothing could be lower. Granted, he was scum as it turned out, but the media's fascination with his occupation was an insult to real fertilizer salesmen. But it is grand sport to point out some alluring interest in an individual who is already on a hot seat for one thing or another and dump it into the story.

Time magazine recognized the journalist's natural instinct to pick out that dimension of a story that was the most titillating when it commented on a disposed candidate for Tom Ridgeway's job as Director of Homeland Security. Time printed: *Maybe when Bernard Kerik decided to try for the Homeland Security Czarship, he figured, "What's the worst that could happen?" How 'bout everything you've ever done wrong appearing on the news, for one?* Kerik was scorched by the media, pointing to his infidelities and other 'bad habits,' etc. His accomplishments as the N.Y. Police Commissioner would have to come later, if at all. It's what we did and do as journalists. Guess what the readers and viewers remember about a story? And considering what has taken place since in New Orleans with Katrina, Kerik might well have been just what we needed. Sometimes, even we wish we weren't so damn right all the time.

The media loves illuminating a long held flaw in some official's character, be it a lie or an ancient stumbling. Many of these people, who get hit by enthusiastic journalists, never recover. They are left to live among the wounded who are periodically reminded by the media of their transgression(s). There are a few exceptions but generally, no matter what contribution he/she has made in the community since, no matter how many times they achieved hero status; no matter what his/her accomplishments might have been…at his/her passing, that old wound will be opened all over again. It reminds not only the viewers and readers of details of something that happened years before but it also puts a damper on the family's pride, comfort and solace of their loss. I nearly got in a fist fight in the newsroom with the producer when once I let an ounce of compassion sweep over me when trying to get the copy changed on the story of a man's demise. I make no apology for having a killer instinct leaving me from time to time.

Never argue with anyone who buys ink by the gallon.
Tommy Lasorda

Like Lasorda says, you may win a battle or two with journalists but never the war. They seem to have time and certainly have the space to wear down the most convincing and most adamant opponent. The truth is that once something gets struck in the craw of a journalist—local or network news operation—there is no spitting it out. They love to savor the taste and swish it around in their mouth until they have sucked every drop of joy juice out of it. Examples run from an individual's misstep to a whole country's misconduct.

Every so often someone comes along and gives the media a swift kick in the ego, but not nearly enough. Most are just too afraid to take on the job. But once in a while an official isn't afraid to bite back. Presidential candidate George Bush (the father, not the son) once responded to a potentially embarrassing question by CBS's Dan Rather by referring to a discomforting but related moment in the anchorman's own life. Rather tried to counter-punch but the swift kick had been delivered. Bush went on to win the election.

Another example is the Tsunami disaster in the Indian Ocean, killing over 175,000 people in Thailand, Sri Lanka and Indonesia, destroying everything in its wake. After a few days, the question was raised that the United States wasn't moving quickly enough in the relief efforts to satisfy the critics. The question was presented to Secretary of State, Colin Powell on a Sunday morning network news interview program. Powell was quick to point out that this was a misleading charge because the U.S. immediately contacted the foreign ministers of the countries involved and President Bush spoke to the Heads of State within 48 hours, and plans were begun within 24 hours of the quake by both government and private organizations to move with efficiency and dispatch.

While the question was still on the lips of some journalists, attention was generally turned to the disaster itself and it became obvious very soon that the U.S. was the leader in providing relief, even having two ex-presidents assigned to coordinate the efforts as well as diverting a division of marine corps troops to the area to help in the clean up. Still, ABC's Diane Sawyer in the area with Secretary Powell found it necessary to lead her questioning of Powell, not with the progress of relief efforts and the continuing life and death struggles, but with the now dated so-called hesitation of the U.S. to get involved with the relief efforts. Powell, with a finely tuned edge in his voice, wasted no time in taking her to task, carefully explaining what the U.S. was doing from the very beginning. Sawyer had no follow up question on the matter, squelching her desire to look like the hard-edged journalist with tough questions. There are times when reporters just have to take their lumps.

3.

You can be absolutely accurate in the information you present, and dead wrong in the impression you leave.

TV news is like a lightning flash.
It makes a loud noise, lights up everything around it ,
leaves everything else in the darkness
and then is suddenly gone.

Hodding Carter

In a way, it's a good thing some people see TV news as a lightning flash. If they truly took the time to examine its many dimensions, the industry would be in big trouble. Too often there is a vague uneasiness about what viewers see and hear on a newscast. Even if they do hear all the words, there are so many visual attractions and *dis*tractions that they have to really be on their toes to be sure the information and impression somehow meet in the middle. And while they're wading through this verbal and visual blitz, there are other factors to consider when marrying the impression with the information, such as *how was the story headlined*? Sometimes the story tease is better than the full story. It's the old National Enquirer trick, and they all use it, some more responsibly than others. *Where also is the story placed in a newscast? How much time is devoted to it?* My mother was sent into frenzy one time when an anchorman read a story on how army engineers were spot-checking dams across the country as purely a safety precaution. A local dam was one to be checked, because of its location...not because anything was wrong. But the visual behind the anchorman was a slide that said *unsafe dams*...plus the fact it was the lead story in the newscast. The other two channels didn't even bother with the story. My mother, however, was convinced something was wrong with the dam. The channel was right with the information and dead wrong in the impression it was leaving. It happens in every newscast, every day.

It takes an unusual skill to walk that line of writing a story that leaves an absolutely accurate *impression* in the mind of the viewer. The newspapers, you say, have the same problem? Of course they do, but newspapers and the other media outlets don't have video, voice emphasis, primary and secondary reading weight, commercial interruptions, teasers (other than headlines) and continuing format changes, among others. Let there be no doubt; television newscasts are a world unto their own. Newspapers, while they have to deal with the owner's political philosophy laced throughout the paper, generally have the space to give a story a full treatment, and in the end give enough information to let the readers develop their own impressions. That is a luxury *viewers* rarely have.

The lightning flash analogy for local TV news seems to fit. The story on television has a brief life between your ears and then it's gone and before you could make any kind of judgment you have *more* information on a totally different subject coming at you to absorb.

On day-to-day coverage, four television stations can cover the same story and each will give it a twist that will differ from the competition. It's a given. Each one will be accurate with its information, but each will leave a different impression. Typically, the problem is how the visual is handled vs. how the copy is written that accompanies it. Another barometer is *placement* in the newscast. Some stations get absolutely giddy with excitement because they have something that no one else has, and no power on earth will stop them from putting it on the air right off the top…even though it doesn't affect anyone's life in any way, shape or form.

Typical of local mentality was gloriously put on display one mid February day in the Salt Lake City market when the biggest story in town, by any standard, was the lifting of an injunction by a federal court, to restart construction on a final 14 mile stretch of something called the Legacy Highway. This one hundred mile stretch of road was to act as a needed corridor through two counties. It was a project mired in controversy and legal entanglements for over three years because that particular stretch went through the Great Salt Lake wetlands, a sensitive nature preserve.

For months on end, highway architects and designers, transportation engineers, lawyers of every stripe, state government and, of course, well represented environmentalists, battled on a daily basis while motorists, job seekers and the public waited for *some* action by *some* court to make *some* decision. Added to the mix was the proposed development of a parkway, and to compound the problem, the highway was being promoted as a piece of art—with designs and structures, the likes of which haven't seen the light of day on a Utah road.

Of course, thousands just wanted to use the highway as a simple transportation and access strip. To say that a lot was at stake is more than a casual understatement. Ultimately, it would affect thousands of lives in Utah as well as make or break reputations and change the character and configuration of large chunks of land. Finally, after 3 ½ years, a decision was made to lift the injunction, allowing construction to begin. Channel Four was so excited about the story it led the newscast with an update of a day old house fire. Channel Two could hardly contain itself by leading the newscast with a story about a moose that wandered onto one of the city's freeway systems. Channel five, on the other hand, stepped away from its usual run of lead stories with flashing red lights and presented remarkable coverage of the highway and its impact on the state and the hundreds of thousands of motorists who would be using it every day. For schools of journalism, there was momentary evidence of a Santa Claus after all.

By starting a newscast with a peripatetic moose on the freeway instead of the approval to finish the conflicted highway that affected millions of people over the years, gives one a glimpse of what is happening to the local news product. It also gives fodder to this *terrible truth* of showing how the impression left doesn't jell with the true importance of the story. Relegating the report behind the moose or a day old fire gives a ho hum nod to the viewer that maybe the damn highway really doesn't matter all that much. Traditionally, there is the attitude that the most important story begins at the top of a TV newscast or as a big headline in the newspaper. But, here again, the question begs…*what is important*…and what criteria is followed when determining what story is more important than another. There are some obvious choices but on a routine day there is no sure fire way to pick the most significant. To the die-hard moose lovers, Channel Two did the right thing. Everything is relative and frankly, I'm spending way too much time even discussing it.

Well, I would—if they realized that we—again…if—if
we led them back to that stalemate only because
that our retaliatory power, our seconds, or strike at them after
our—first strike, would be so destructive that they
couldn't afford it, that would hold them off.

President Reagan
when asked if nuclear war could
be limited to tactical weapons

The President, with his unofficial title of… "The Great Communicator," had to join a long list of people who blew it while on TV trying to say something profound or reasonably intelligent. The best of them falter and fall at times. But because news never forgets, presidents and plumbers alike are at the mercy of the insidious minds of the journalists and producers. Once a subject answers a question, it is best not to elaborate or embellish too much. The odds of screwing up by saying something stupid, unforgettable or unforgivable are astonishingly high. Only the hottest comment, the dumbest answer or the most contorted look, make the cut. Politicians pay for their sins again and again by the replay of some old stupid comment made at the worst possible time. What they fear is real; replaying a year old piece can change an impression *and* a vote.

In the real world,
the right thing never happens in the right way at the right time.
It is the job of journalists and historians
to make it appear that it has.

Mark Twain

This Twain remark is a two edged sword. He is suggesting that journalists fudge a little on the information—which is done too often anyway—and then he is assuming the journalist is smart enough to align the information to make it more enticing and palatable, making it even more impressive but hardly accurate. This is scarcely a reassuring quote for the viewer, or worse, the subject of an interview. Whatever the material content, the editor's heavy hand can arrange the video to show the up or downside of someone's performance or concentrate on the most unattractive feature in a room. The selection process can reinforce someone's position or make him look like a damn fool. The hope is that the decision will rest with a responsible, unbiased, fair minded, objective editor/reporter. These days, it's a roll of the dice as to what piece of video will make it on the air.

History and *accuracy* sometimes play second fiddle to momentary amusement. Producers may even decide to resurrect some old video that reminds the subject —mostly politicians—of some foot-in-the-mouth comment they made weeks, months or even years before. Creating an accurate impression to match the information being presented these days is a full time job. And as sure as a five year old will mispronounce *aluminum*, the two rarely match.

> *Letterman is a smart guy*
> *who can spot a phony with telescopic accuracy.*
> Bill O'Reilly 2006

Bill O'Reilly, a conservative commentator on FOX News may have wanted to eat those words after he was challenged by David Letterman of CBS's Late Night Show who told him that 60% of his comments were "crap." And, of course, that is the cut that was used ad infinitum by news and other talk shows the next day. Dressing down O'Reilly is probably great sport in today's information atmosphere but was the impression made on the viewers fair to O'Reilly? The bigger question, you say, may be, *"Since when did 'fair' become a part of journalism's vocabulary?"* If the whole sequence between Letterman and O'Reilly—instead of a single bite—was watched by impartial viewers, another impression of O'Reilly may emerge. While making a few thrusts of his own, O'Reilly made a decent accounting of himself. Overall, Letterman was quite respectful of O'Reilly and the pair parted amiably. But forever more that one comment by Letterman will be played over and over again and will hang like a millstone around O'Reilly's neck.

Another example of selective editing was with Howard Dean, a presidential candidate in 2004 and later the Democratic National Chairman. His presidential bid was essentially snuffed out when responding to a defeat in Iowa in front of a crowd of noisy supporters. He yelled. He shouted. He frantically waved his arms. He punched the air. In general, he looked like a man on a rant, desperate to be heard. Of course this little episode was played and replayed repeatedly on every channel in every city. Perhaps Dean was over the edge, however, ABC News, to its credit, demonstrated what was happening in the room from the point of view of both Dean and his supporters.

Dean, as it turned out, was using a special broadcast microphone that greatly muffled the extraneous noise around him, which just happened to be very energetic, very loud, very sustained. Dean was unaware of this feature on his mike, so to his own ears he felt he had to shout over top of the clamorous crowd to be heard, hoping to rally his supporters in the face of this recent defeat. ABC's Good Morning America clearly confirmed the noise level Dean had to overcome to get his message across. The ABC mike, *without* the noise reduction feature, demonstrated the frustration any candidate would have to overcome to keep his supporters in line, in this case, showing Dean to be just very enthusiastic instead of an out of control maniac. But the damage to him in the late evening news and the days ahead was complete. President of the U.S. would not be on Dean's resume anytime soon.

Dean and O'Reilly are only a few of a few thousand people who have had their best stuff land on the cutting room floor, to use a tired old Hollywood cliché. This is a condition that has been very prevalent over the past decade and it will only get worse. As technology develops an even sharper edge, any person in the country can pull up clips of everything that has ever been on TV, from Andy Griffith 50 years ago to last night's news. Nothing is sacred and every flaw and every embarrassing moment will forever be kept in a hermetically sealed vault to be taken out in time to make someone look like a jackass all over again, or make him explain to an aggressive reporter an earlier controversial comment. However, the golden moments of man's better nature will be stored away too but they'll probably atrophy from disinterest. Helping people make a favorable impression is not one of journalism's stronger virtues.

One would think that there would be a viewer uprising over all the sunshine the media is trying to pump up their derriere, but rarely is there a complaint about coverage, style, placement, graphics, etc. But that isn't to say they are happy about the way we do things. Sometimes viewers just need a reason to express themselves. It happened once with great gusto during the Nixon administration when Vice President Spiro Agnew gave a speech in Alabama. He referred to the TV journalists as *'nattering nabobs of negativity.'* We scurried to the dictionary to determine what we had been called… and according to Webster; we were *important people who like to endlessly scold others.* Everyone knew the Vice President was echoing President Nixon's attitude toward the press.

We all may have laughed at the description of being *nabobs* but our amusement was short-lived. Our phones started ringing and, almost without exception, the viewers fully supported Mr. Agnew. I'm not sure they really knew what *"nattering nabobs"* were but it sounded bad enough to make a call. My favorite was from a gentleman responding to a story we'd done about someone who had done something out of the ordinary. He accused us of subtly lacing the report with innuendo and absence of fact. Well, we've been accused of a lot of things but *being subtle* is not one of them. First of all, the viewer should have looked up the word in the dictionary. And secondly, it's not easy being subtle no matter how you define it. Journalists are by nature like a bull in a China closet. The idea of being subtle rarely crosses a reporter's keyboard. The fact is that most of us probably aren't sharp enough to be subtle enough to cleverly sabotage anyone. If it actually happens, it is generally done out of ignorance and incompetence. We are not Horace Greeley, H.V. Kaltenborn or even Edward R. Murrow. Even if we were bright enough to be subtle in our writing, we don't have the time, knack or space to do it. We hack out our stories in record time in a noisy newsroom with producers yelling for our copy, the anchorman changing it to fit his/her style, the director yelling for the scripts for blocking and your wife/husband is calling to remind you to bring home a bag of pampers. Subtle indeed. It's as hard *to be* subtle as it is to spell the damn word in the first place. (*The silent B has thrown more than one student of the profession.*)

Taking criticism is not an easy thing to do, in any chosen profession. In journalism, one of the main things we have to keep in mind—particularly when high officials like the Vice President of the United States spends a whole speech on it—is not to overreact. It can either numb our senses or make reporters more insensitive than ever. The one protective shield we have is *The Truth*. There is no doubt that viewers get offended at times because some reporters go for the jugular when it isn't always necessary…and will sometimes even offend those who aren't a part of the story. A reporter is used to wearing protective armor and contrary to charges made against them, most try *not* to overreact but continue an aggressive stance against those who subvert the public trust or the laws of the land. Journalists do like to make a point and some do it very well, but they will deny they are overreacting.

When I was seventeen years old I saw a classic case of overreaction which lives with me today. Northeastern Montana is not exactly a Mecca for tourists but can be a quick road stop for a weary traveler. And it isn't one of those places where celebrities buy up property and join hands with Mother Nature to enjoy the good life. Most of the towns along what is called the Montana Highline are small wheat producing communities, 20-30 miles apart that follow the Great Northern Railroad on U.S. Highway 2. It's a two-lane road that caters to local commerce, truckers, business travel, in state, and to a lesser degree, out-of-state tourist travel. But it's enough to keep a reasonable amount of traffic on the road for small service stations, motels and cafés to survive.

My mom and step-dad, Grant, owned a Texaco service station in Saco. Nothing fancy, just a mom and pop business with a small office and nothing else for a traveler to buy except oil and gas products. No concrete, just gravel and dirt on both sides of the two gas pumps.

One evening, about dusk, while mom worked the books, Grant and I serviced the intermittent flow of customers. Grant had had a few drinks by the time a lone driver pulled up to the pumps late in the afternoon. No self-service in those days. I went to the front of the car and raised the hood to check the water and oil. Grant grabbed the hose and started filling the gas tank. These days, car gas tanks and the pumps themselves generally have a physical system that stops gas from backing up and splashing back on the person filling the tank...but not then. Grant, with liquid in his own tank, carelessly put a little bit too much pressure on the nozzle and, bingo, a very small amount of gas splashed back and onto the ground. Grant adjusted, wiped what little gas got on the car fender and finished filling the tank. When he told the guy...*'That'll be $6.00'*...the guy says...*'Hell, you've got fifty cents worth of gas on the ground!'*

I was still under the hood and heard the exchange...and knowing Grant's condition I feared the worst. In a very calculating way and with a very measured tone in his voice, Grant said quietly...*'You want to see what fifty cents worth of gas looks like on the ground?'* The man, at this point, was stuck for a comment...and I could see it coming, but before I could stop it, Grant turned the nozzle away from the car and gas pumps and proceeded to pump fifty cents worth of gas on the ground, then pulled out a stick match from his overalls, lit it with his thumbnail and tossed it into the middle of the small lake. As a rapidly developing blaze lit up the Western sky, Grant, with a slight smile, turned to the man and said…*"THAT'S fifty cents worth of gas on the ground!"* The man quickly pulled six bucks out of his wallet, handed it over without a word, quickly got in his car and drove off with the fire still burning in his rear view mirror. If he is alive today I'm sure he is telling this tale to his grandkids for the tenth time. There's a point to remember when contemplating this story. In those days, gas was only 32 cents for a full gallon. Do the math and you'll figure out the size of the fire. Today, fifty cents' worth would barely wet the ground.

I think of this story often. Did Grant overreact? Of course! He could have blown up the station if there were fumes rising to the open air from the tanks below. Did he make his point? Absolutely! Journalists only wish their points were as dramatic and absolute. Some reporters will go overboard to find and hold on to a definitive statement in a story.

By the very nature of the journalism industry there is always more information that can be put into our mental tanks on any story. Some reporters are just too lazy to ferret it out while others pursue a story to a point where it loses its punch when too much irrelevant information is presented. But it isn't generally the journalist that recognizes it. It is the viewer who has had it with much ado about nothing. Some reporters get so attached to a story that they think everyone must feel the same way. Over reacting is a common ailment among the industry's faithful, whether an inside story in Washington D.C., over who leaked what to whom, or a feud between the mayor and a city councilman in Butte, Montana. Competent editing in the newsroom is always the wiser course. The producer of a local newscast has to balance what is important, against what else has happened that day.

Granted, there are some days when an inordinate amount of time is given a story that doesn't mean squat to the people or the community, but because of some great film/tape footage the producer shortens more important stories to show all the pretty pictures. If there had been a television news crew passing through Saco when Grant torched the lake of gas, it would have led the newscast in Great Falls, not to mention that it would also lead to the ultimate arrest of Grant for endangering a community and the Texaco Oil Company taking away his dealership. What doesn't get reported on a daily basis around the country, big city or small town is phenomenal. A pitifully small slice of the pie is served to the media to report or exploit.

63

I hate to leave Grant standing there watching that lake of gas on fire without acknowledging some of the more pleasant memories in my life. There were good times. He was just a product of his own background and times when making a living was a never-ending struggle. He did have a few passions in his life, besides the bottle. Another was one of the most popular female movie stars at the time, Ginger Rogers. He tried to see all her movies and read whatever he could about her. Years later, as luck would have it; Ms. Rogers was in Salt Lake City promoting some cosmetic that had her name on it. She was obviously well past her prime and out of the public eye, at least for anyone younger than 50. When she came into the station, I made sure I did the radio interview with her. After we finished I told her how much my step-dad adored her movies and always talked about her but lamented the fact his chances of seeing her in the flesh were a billion to one. To her great credit, Ms. Rogers said…*"Let's call him on the phone right now."* It was hard to hold back a tear or two when I had to tell her that he had passed away three weeks before. If his heart had held out, that phone call would have kept him alive another ten years. Either that or kill him on the spot.

> *Whether it's the best of times or the worst of times,*
> *it's the only time we've got.*
> Art Buchwald

…and journalists function in whatever time it is. For them the best and worst of times are generally one and the same. To them, time is a reference point, not ticks on a clock. Stories generally happen when it is the most inconvenient, not in a tidy eight-hour period from nine to five. For the reporter, the worst of times is when he doesn't have enough time to properly cover and prepare a story, leaving out important information. It is the failure to see the central point of a story, or the lack of research or being lazy in the reporting process or just plain poor writing that gets us into trouble by presenting an improper impression.

As earlier mentioned, the viewer flatters us when he calls us "subtle." Generally, we ain't that dazzling. While there are a chosen few who can write circles around their fellow journalists, most of us couldn't get a job at the newspaper if we tried to bribe the managing director. Our writing is so different that we forget how a *real journalist* does it. It isn't until someone from the newspaper crosses over to television that we find out how to really write a story…and then, incredibly, we can't use it because it doesn't fit the style, drama or technique of *writing for the visual* that accompanies the reporter or anchor's script. Maybe we aren't as bad as we sometimes think.

Making an impression that is accurate for the viewer, as mentioned, is no walk in the park. Journalists do their best to correctly describe an event or an individual. But there are those rare times when the subject is so challenging that even the impression created on the reporter makes it next to impossible to muster up enough energy to complete a story. Ironically, my albatross was a man so honored, so accomplished, so heroic, so fearless that it would be folly for any journalist to hint at anything wrong with his character or personality. He is a man who has looked death in the eye more times then the rest of us can imagine. And yet, he proved to me that he can be the biggest horse's ass in the universe. Simply stated, I have never met a more contrary man.

Chuck Yeager shook my hand when I extended it, but made no comment when I told him I enjoyed his book. He immediately turned his head and wandered away. He was in an Orem, Utah factory, owned by a man (Sam), who had met him at some gathering and then invited him to come to Utah as a forerunner to a hunting and fishing trip in Canada, a passion of Yeager's. But first, Sam had asked him to pose by his company's product, and then later in the day to talk to a gathering of Boy Scouts. Sam, a scout leader himself, thought it would be a nice fit for Yeager because of his own early membership in the scouts as a youth. Waiting for the photographer to arrive, Yeager refused an interview as well as engage in meaningless conversation with any of the 7 or 8 people in the area. One was supposed to be a surprise to Yeager, his roommate at flight school in the early forties. The guy had been bragging all his life about knowing Yeager and just wanted to get a picture of the two of them together, now in their senior years. He had even brought along a picture of the two of them in flight school. Yeager shook the guy's hand but had no interest in the old picture and refused to have a new one taken, though the man had a camera of his own for the occasion. Further, Yeager rebuffed any attempt at dialogue with his old classmate. The man, who had brought his grown son along, was left standing as Yeager wandered off in another direction. Embarrassed, they left. When Sam told Yeager the man was terminally ill, he just said, "We all die." Later that evening, Yeager managed to offend the parents and scouts with his attitude, apathy and impudence, many leaving before the program was over. And the church involved has put out the word that Yeager will not be permitted to use their facilities to talk with scouts for whatever reason.

Now, how do I report such a story? Bashing a hero of three wars isn't exactly the most popular approach. And there is nothing I could say that would alter his behavior. When you have *"slipped the surly bonds of earth…and touched the face of God" there's* not much of anything that anyone can do to you. So, I did nothing. Somehow, matching the impression with the accuracy of the story didn't seem so important. I was a wiser but sadder man.

> *I believe in equality for everyone,*
> *except reporters and photographers*
> Mahatma Ghandi

Even the great Ghandi wasn't one to make a fuss over reporters. He too had felt the sting from their writings. I'm almost sure he is resting comfortably knowing not only of his impact on the world but the fact he didn't have to be interviewed by a Mike Wallace.

To acknowledge and honor a reporter's work is as rare as Native Americans initiating a tribute to George Armstrong Custer. Since the journalist works on the darker side of the street it is difficult to find enough people to pay him an appropriate acknowledgment. Praising the messenger of information, a la, the journalist, is generally limited to comments between friends over drinks than some public display of affection and appreciation. Reporters, producers and anchors are like Greyhound bus drivers; they are doing what is expected of him, nothing more or less. They handle bumps in the road and a winding, narrow highway with expected expertise. And like the bus driver there are occasional lapses for which a price may be paid. For the journalist anyway, recognition of his/her work must come from *within* the industry itself. One critic likened this self-hurrah to a gathering of dung beetles to celebrate the one that has produced the biggest dung ball. As such, the dung beetle is not unlike its human counterpart who is not timid about where they find their subject material.

If you want to be loved and adored by the public, consider nursing, charity work, architecture, plumbing, glass blowing, *anything* but being a journalist. Reporters, producers, correspondents, columnists and commentators are accepted and even needed and sometimes, in a rare mood, people will even nod approvingly of their work, but generally readers and viewers always withhold their affection and respect. If journalism is your choice of professions and you work diligently at your craft and hold out hope for some positive public acknowledgment of your celebrated effort, relax—it would be simpler to teach your cat to meow the National Anthem. If you want to convince John Q. and his wife that your work demands their blessing, talk instead to your priest, rabbi, minister, bishop or mahatma.

Thankfully, journalists take criticism in stride, disapproval being an occupational hazard. They also know they are an important cog in the necessary flow of information. The problem is that too often, they are both the messenger and the message, thereby confusing the public, irritating their own kind, ignoring an ethical code or aborting their own set standards of verification. Meanwhile, John and Suzie Schwartz in the quiet of their living room are being fed a daily dose of television news that reporters make themselves believe is an essential, even an indispensable element to help John and Suzie *make* decisions and *gather* knowledge needed to enrich their lives. Further, it is to *provide* information to satisfy their curiosity, *assembles* data to give credence to the admonition to be well informed, and *collects* facts to assist them in a hundred different ways. So what if there are a few dung balls along the way. That's life in any profession. The journalist just sticks his or her efforts out there in the open for everyone to see, probe, smell, examine, kick, criticize, swallow or choke on.

However the information might be handled, in one-way or another, life is mirrored on every newscast everyday. For the reporter or producer, on any given day or on any given subject, it isn't easy to be fully accurate, straightforward, unattached, appropriately compassionate, fair and equal, inoffensive, balanced, unbiased and accurate with the impression they leave behind. Talk to any mother trying to raise a child.

As for examining the subject of journalism itself and its presentation, as well as those who also labor within its borders—everyone of every stripe, from plumbers to prostitutes, seem to have something to say, many speaking from the gut while others use an open mind and plenty of viewing experience. Still others take out a microscope and examine every nuance, every fact, and every attribution or lack thereof. It is a murky profession and certainly should be probed with every necessary tool. But while wielding that sharp edged knife it would be well to remember what both local and national news say they are trying to do *for* and *to* us; namely, to illuminate what we *need* to know, what we *should* know and give us enough information to form opinions about our world and our neighborhood. Some of that information is supposed help us make decisions that will affect our lives, hopefully in a positive way. Some of it is just plain information that has some peripheral interest to our own existence, about how we are lucky not to be involved in some accident or flu epidemic or make us understand that our lives are often just a roll of the dice.

> *You want to talk about the news, the news business, the way we* ***want*** *it to be, the way we'd* ***like*** *it to be, the way—in theory— the way it* ***ought*** *to be…or do you want to talk about the* ***real*** *world?"*
>
> Sam Donaldson
>
> ABC News

Sam Donaldson, the network news equivalent of Mac the Knife, often may be over the edge to some, but I'd suggest you hold off debating him about the business. No one is more of a realist than Sam. He knows that as long as men and women have a pencil and paper, a camera or microphone...nothing is secure. Nothing is safe. Nothing is private. That is the nature of the profession, just as it is to inform, explain and educate.

A journalist also likes to talk out of school and find that one dimension that will sell his/her story to the public. Viewers can talk all they want about wanting responsible journalism to be broadcast into their homes, but they also have shown an incredible proclivity to hear and see the side of a story that is part of society's underbelly. Viewers also seem to readily accept that reporters often appear to be more obsessed with celebrity than culture, fantasy over fact, political faux pas in place of legislative good works, controversy instead of thoughtful and solid debate, achievement being trumped by tragedy ...and what *could* or *should be* instead of *what is*. It is simply the way local boys and girls of journalism play the game.

In the latter part of 2005, two Democratic legislators issued statements about the war in Iraq. Representative John Murtha's wanted U.S. Forces to withdraw from Iraq and during the same period of time Senator Joe Lieberman said we must stand fast, pointing to "real progress." Almost to a man, the news media geared up and trumpeted Murtha's call from sea to shining sea. Lieberman was barely a blip on the radar. Syndicated columnist, Kathleen Parker, posed the question of why one side was covered extensively and the other was virtually ignored. Lieberman, she noted, had just returned from his fourth trip to Iraq and discussed the consequences of prematurely withdrawing U.S. Troops. *"And why, we might wonder,"* she said, *"have the media—always so insistent in denying the liberal bias—been so willing to play one story and not another? I'm just askin."* Depending on party affiliation, most people might want to ask the same question.

Whether national, international or local…viewers will always ask questions. As such, there is simply no explaining the motives behind much of what the media does. It is one reason the viewer or reader must make his/her own decisions based on all the material available and not let the media make the decisions for them. TV news is *not* the voice of the people. It is a conveyer of information that has to be checked against other media outlets when the issues at hand are particularly sensitive.

News: an aberration from normalcy.

Charlie Cook
National Journal

Telling the media what to cover and how to cover it has been an ongoing game for as long as there have been reporters, readers, listeners and viewers. And it is a game that will continue for as long as Halley's Comet continues to make its rounds. In March, 2006, President Bush was holding a town meeting and fielding questions from the citizens. One woman asked why the news was so negative about Iraq and why some of the progress isn't reported more frequently. The audience burst into sustained applause. The President also nodded approvingly. The media, on the other hand, shrugged its shoulders and went about its business. "It is," says Charlie Cook, "…*the nature of news.*" Cook goes on to say that a reporter can get killed going out to look for good news in Iraq, a sobering fact that was all too true.

*Some stories are a product **of** the media*
*and **by** the media, if not just **for** the media.*
Tom Wicker

The idea of being accurate with information and yet leave a false impression was a concept in the making by a local TV station that had hired a hotshot investigative reporter from another station in another state. One of the points he made with management was *to pick a state agency that caters to several people where there is a considerable amount of money being spent on vague services.* So when a phone call came in to a reporter at the TV station-in-question from a disgruntled employee at the Utah State Training School about the facility being untidy and with some of the residents being abused, the investigative team was ready to pounce. Ideal agency, ideal situation, a scattering of ideal targets and ideal people who were defenseless and harmless…and ideal attendants who were overworked and underpaid…and best of all, it was a rating period. The reporting team had grabbed the brass ring…and Tom Wicker was right on the money.

The Utah State Training School was an institution for the mentally retarded or *mentally challenged* as we prefer these days. Even in the best of times this was a difficult facility to manage and impossible to service all the resident's needs… and harder still to find responsible, competent, dedicated people to work in the several buildings devoted to the care of both children and adults.

I watched, with particular interest, the five part series that featured 28 specific charges against the School. The residents numbered about 600…one of which was my daughter, Kristin. I knew the School, the residents, the management and the attendants as no other reporter in the state. My advantage was that I was now an independent and could act on my own.

It was a tense time in the Governor's office. One of the state's largest departments (Social Services) was taking a major hit. Because of my experience in TV News and because my daughter was a resident, the Governor put me in charge of a panel to investigate the charges. Of the 28, not a single allegation stood up and we even took it from the viewpoint of the TV station.

Like it happens so often when a station is doing investigating reporting, only the surface bad is given emphasis, while the reasons behind it are ignored because it would soften the accusation. For instance…one of the charges dealt with the Thanksgiving Day meal. The station said…*"…the meal the residents were given late in the afternoon consisted of sandwiches of peanut butter and jelly and lunch meat.* What the station failed to report was the content of the *other* meal—turkey (all you could eat), cranberries, pumpkin pie, dressing, milk and fruit juices, potatoes and gravy (two kinds), corn on the cob, hot buns, butter, jam…and two flavors of ice cream. I don't know about the rest of the world but after a meal like that, I'd be set for three days. Plus the school told the residents that left over turkey was available upon request. PB&J sandwiches indeed! The other charges against the school had similar stories of omission behind them, though basically accurate on the information they did present…but terribly wrong on the impression left behind.

Also…a film presentation was produced illuminating the vast differences between truth and fantasy and was presented to the state legislature…and to the credit of the offending station's ownership, ½ hour was set aside to air the program in a prime time slot. The end result was that no parent removed their child from the school, the school continued to get its yearly allotment of funds, my daughter continued to receive her usual tender and loving care…and the investigative reporter moved out of town two months later.

This may sound like a self-serving episode in my life but it happens with regularity all over the country. Investigative reporting is all too often an *us against them* kind of scenario with un-named sources, clandestine meetings, rifling through files without permission, undercover observations, etc. The problem is that too many times a reporter doesn't go far enough because he/she might find something positive that would negate the thrill of the chase.

There is an old strategy in war, voiced by former Secretary of Defense, Robert McNamara that would well serve the investigative reporter. *"Empathize with your enemy." Know what they are doing and why, what their thought process happens to be, what is motivating them, what do they expect to gain, how much are they willing to lose, what part of their game plan is hidden?*

Granted, when theft, greed, etc. are highly suspected, move with dispatch. But if you think you can embarrass someone make sure you think everything through to the finish. If the hand is not in the till or there is no body, and all you have to go on is gossip, hearsay, or a disgruntled employee, proceed with caution. Fabrication is not a tool of a responsible reporter. Some of the largest papers in the country and notable television stations have been hoodwinked by reporters with visions of grandeur. A single individual can destroy the reputation of a paper or a TV news department.

> *People don't always recognize bad writing,*
> *but they will, eventually, become vaguely uncomfortable*
> *and turn away.*
>
> *Harry Reasoner*
> CBS/ABC News

This Reasoner admonishment is one that every reporter should be spoon-fed every day. We sometimes forget the public's intelligence. Sloppy writing can, indeed, make people turn away. It is through slipshod writing that can sink a story, or more likely, lessen its impact on the viewer. It can also change the impression of what the visual is trying to establish and that can be undeserved, not only to the story, but the viewer as well.

We had a running philosophy in the news room that we tried to believe was true even though we were barely conscious of it when producing our stories; *give the people accurate, understandable information to let them know what is going on in their community and world…and provide stories they can relate to…and, at times, even help them make important decisions in their lives.* A little over the top maybe, but who knows, at times, we may have done just that.

4.

Contrary to its own promotion, a local TV newscast is not the voice of the people or even an accurate reflection of the community.

A community needs a soul
if it is to become a true home for human beings.
You, the people, must give it this soul.
Pope Paul II

A thing is right when it tends to
preserve the integrity, stability and beauty
of the living community.
It is wrong when it tends otherwise.
Aldo Leopold 1887-1948

You can't discuss news—electronic or print—without involving the community. Whatever we do or say or write or film or tape is done on behalf of the community. Admittedly, the idea of *not* being "a voice of the people," after years of trying to convince viewers otherwise, is both disturbing and challenging. *Disturbing* because the people aren't necessarily getting what the media say they are providing…and *challenging* because the media feel some guilt in not closely recognizing and presenting a stronger, more accurate view of the community.

Pope Paul II and Aldo Leopold, aptly describe the importance of *community* to its citizens and the need to hold the *community* to a high standard. But building that standard is another matter and one of the main alliances should be the media making a conscious effort to examine areas that need more attention. This book is not a forum for what the media should or shouldn't do. It is just about a *terrible truth* that the media, particularly TV news from which the viewer gets most of his information, has frayed edges and doesn't have the knowledge, money, time or manpower to do justice to community needs. Instead, viewers get only an overview of something serious, something frivolous or something meaningless, though a feast for the eyes. Even stories that have an impact with the viewers generally don't provide enough information to make a full judgment on their content.

In 1902—before voice and pictures could be transmitted through the air…and before Brian Williams was a twinkle in his father's eye, journalist Finley Peter Dunne observed that journalism had a unique capacity to *comfort the afflicted and afflict the comfortable*. This catchy but overused statement doesn't begin to tell the story of journalism… and does, in fact, tell precious little of it. The same Mr. Dunne was a highly regarded author of his time but like Shaw, he had an itch to scratch with his own kind. He also rattled on about how newspapers did everything for us, claiming they influenced police action… and how they put pressure on banks, the legislature and the military. For good measure, he accused journalists of having a hand in baptizing the young, marrying the foolish, burying the dead and roasting him afterward. Dunne was also one of the first to say that…*There ain't any news in being good,* and…*Don't jump on a man unless he is down.*

A few generations later, the same attitude is still around and is further tarnished by the most flawed opinion ever perpetrated on the journalist or the people— *The public has a right to know!* We'll discuss it later for it overlaps a few of the terrible truths.

Some of Dunne's spirit lives today and seems to be a guiding light for a few of today's more aggressive journalists. And what the newspapers might have forgotten since Dunne's day, television has taken up the slack with stories that are noisier, bloodier, flashier, sexier…and surrounded with more color, off the wall graphics and anchors that make it sound like they can read the fine print off a mortgage contract and make you feel good about it. And now, because of people's vanishing habit of routinely reading the newspaper, the road is paved for the electronic boys and girls to broadcast the news in a way that panders to management, compromises the newsroom, satisfies the consultants, and has the production values of a Follies Bergere, all the while short changing the viewer. Finley Dunne must be twisting in his grave for having missed all the fun.

TV news in particular follows a course that brings in the most viewers, a course that concentrates on drama instead of the quality of the information it presents. Further, the viewer is only treated to bits and pieces of the community, just occasionally going into depth…and is swept along with a news operation reacting more to the flashing red lights instead of the quiet steady white light on efforts being made to build the community. Then throw in those two cousins called controversy and profit to really complicate things.

Generally speaking, what seems to be terribly important in a newsroom is only mildly interesting in the living room. I know this is a shock to a newsroom where reporters, videographers, editors and management actually believe they are presenting an accurate reflection of their community. Reporters can spend their days living and dying with stories they sometimes think should rock our world; more likely, a newscast is a suggestion of not only of what happened that day, but the mood, temperament, interest and character of the assignment editor, the producer and the reporter.

After a nightly newscast, a huge percentage of the homes turn off the station or watch a late night show without another thought of what was on the newscast. At the same time, in the newsroom, everyone is still a little giddy and self congratulatory for breaking a particular story or providing spectacular footage of something, or revealing a hidden agenda in the Governor's office or obtaining an elusive interview. And well they should. But the next day the viewer won't remember what story was broken or who shot the footage or what the footage was about or what was going on in the Governor's office or who did what interview with whom. It is simply the nature of the business of both the newscast and the viewer. Of course there are always exceptions, when something is presented that captivates for days on end. To truly capture the continuing mood of a community, you have to be in sync with every soul *in* the community and that, of course, is impossible. Intuitively, everyone in the community knows the kind of city, town or village they live in and its more troubling issues. However, the bigger the community, the more complex the concerns and the more fragmented the interest of the population. Clearly, a huge chunk of the community is not always listening and responding to the dictates of a few newscasts. When they do, it is because there was an examination of an issue that hits home—but, again, not everyone's home.

Granted, the community *is* the gristmill for TV news departments. It is the reporter's job to accurately cover what is happening that is of public interest. *Public interest* is the tricky part. If all the local TV reporters truly understood what the term meant they might have more than only the fifty percent of the people in their viewing area actually watch them do what they are suppose to do. Oh, they do cover those obvious stories that walk in their front door—the accidents and conspicuous crime—but fall painfully short of examining a critical concern of the community.

The defining difference between the reporting stations comes when they do their 'in-depth' material —either the story behind the story or an investigation of an issue. It is in these areas where stations can occasionally excel, if the planets are aligned properly. It is also what most of their promotion is about. But then the bigger the story and the more personalities involved, the rougher the reporting terrain. It is here where experience, talent, patience, resources and money come home to roost. The stations are not, unfortunately, always up to the challenge. The public isn't asking them to be Woodward & Bernstein every night…but they expect competent reporting of what the hell is truly going on in their communities and *of what* they should be aware.

It's effortless to be critical of a news operation. At one time or another everyone takes their shot. Sometimes it's fair and deserved, but not always.
At a glance, no matter how brief the relationship between the newscast, the viewers and the community, it is not a connection made in the stars. No matter how conscientious a news department or the interest level of the viewer or the need in the community, there is only a rare chance the three will agree upon what is said or carried out, each having conflicting priorities on a daily basis.

For all the conflicts, real or perceived, the news operation of a TV station is always in the catbird seat. In the end it will do whatever it damn well wants. And generally, what it wants most is a growing audience. Unfortunately, too often viewers will settle for the news that is easiest to cover—the accidents, crime crap and the stuff that is scheduled and predictable. And a TV news operation tries not to let any of these stories slip through their fingers. Carl Bernstein reminds us that…*the greatest felony in the news business is to be behind, or to miss a big story. But speed substitutes for thoroughness, quality and accuracy.* Amen to that.

> *"A newscast must have action in the first 12 seconds.*
> *And it doesn't matter what the action is."*
> Don Hewett
> Producer, 60 Minutes

Even though I thought our newscasts were fast and snappy, I still felt we were being fairly comprehensive in airing information that would keep the viewers well informed. After living a good portion of my life in a TV newsroom I thought I was in tune and in touch with most everything people had to deal with on a daily basis. It wasn't until I left that newsroom cocoon that I realized what the 'real world' was like. Information I thought was important suddenly had very little meaning for me…and other data that dictated my family's every step in life became very real and outside the parameters of a news room. It's no news bulletin to most local journalists that living and working in the work-a-day world is a hell of a lot different than covering it. The mortgage still has to be paid, stupid people still get in your way, the neighbor's dog still barks too loud, interest rates still break your back, big corporations still make you dance to their music, legislators still pass unpopular laws, community agencies still battle against the odds to do good things and individuals are still vulnerable to pressures from within and without.

If the philosophy of that newsroom had a stronger allegiance to how a community operates instead of being obsessed with that *"12 seconds of action,"* there just might be a day when the newscast matches its promotion. Of course this would necessitate that the reporter work harder and smarter, be more creative and present information in a way to keep viewers interested in what they are saying. This may also take patience on the part of management who may also have to show as much commitment to the community as they do to advertising revenue.

Granted, there are those occasional stories that go beneath the surface and in some small way, evoke some action or change. And of course, you can bet the promotion department will be talking about it well before the stories are scheduled to air. Sadly, those considered the most interesting are generally saved for the rating periods. Still, very few stories hit home with the impact needed to move someone to action. A local politician who cheated on his expense report or has a personal crisis may dominate the airwaves for a week, but doesn't mean a thing to me and mine. It doesn't affect my paycheck or how I do my business or determine what car, house or jellyroll donut I'll buy. It may be an interesting story to some, but my grandson had a ball game to play and I didn't have time to watch television…even if the story did lead the newscast.

Every newscast consists of the same amount of time,
whether there is any news in it or not.
Henry Fielding

There seems to be a lot of folks who like to take a shot at what is and isn't news. We discussed this in the *First Terrible Truth* but it is a subject that will forever be debated by both journalists and readers, viewers and listeners…and none will ever be totally right *or* totally wrong. It must be said however, that some subjects fascinate a news operation much *longer* than they fascinate the recipients who must endure the coverage.

If there is something going on in the community to a level where everyone is talking about it, you can bet it was the media that uncovered the original story and just won't give it up. The more they pump it, the more people talk about it, particularly if there was nothing else going on elsewhere in the community. And therein lies the rub. How much information is presented is predicated on what else is happening. Sadly, if there has been nothing going on, some stories will drag on longer than is necessary and if a lot is going on, something or someone is going to be shortchanged. And then there are those times when the subject of a story gets lucky.

Remember the popular married U.S. Senator who drove off a bridge with a lady who was not his wife and she died as a result? It happened the same day Neil Armstrong stepped on the moon. This is an extreme and obvious case but does demonstrate the priorities the news media have to deal with on a daily basis. The senator barely made the news and for days afterwards he was relegated to page 2 or 3 in the newspaper…and in the second section of news on television. If not for Armstrong, the senator would have been the *only* thing on page one or on the first half of a television broadcast. Of course, the news did catch up to him, in spades…but the bloom was already off the rose.

The idea in news is basic; if there is nothing else going on, wring every last drop of blood, sweat, tears, juice, irony, controversy or scandal out of whatever is tantalizing at the moment, whether its tragic, hilarious or a new hitch in an old story. Believe me, if the media had better things to do, they'd move on and so would the viewers. If the media had left a story alone, nobody would have given it a second thought. Their coverage gives the story "legs" far beyond what it probably deserves. The newsroom doesn't say it in so many words but they like to do the viewers' thinking for them…and the viewers allow it to happen.

So the obvious comment is…*so what?* What does this have to do with anything? Actually, most of the time, nothing! The news operation tells it like it is…and the viewer is kind enough to watch and sometimes respond. Each has a responsibility to the other. The anticipation of each is generally beyond expectations, up or down. Over or under-kill is always a concern on every story. Selection and execution of a story play their own roles. *Just why are we doing this story in the first place? The other channels aren't covering it, etc.* And the viewer may say, *big deal,* or, *so what,* or, *I didn't know that,* or, *wow,* or, *crap, enough already,* or, *I hate the way the anchor combs his/her hair* or, *How much longer before the weather,* etc. In the end, it's a standoff with each of them enduring and sometimes even enjoying the other.

> *There is only one absolute truth I have learned in the hotel business.*
> *It is better to have the shower curtain on the inside of the tub*
> *than the outside.*
>
> Conrad Hilton, Founder
> Hilton Hotel chain.

Truth can be an elusive quality at times. Yet occasionally, it is right under our noses. It's not always as obvious as Mr. Hilton's truth, but the lesson here is that all things don't have to be so complicated. Journalists find that *truth* in their investigations sometimes hides in plain site. In our anxiety to tell an accurate story we may be trying too hard and even sometimes find a simple truth concealed in the normal flow of information at our disposal.

I had always thought I had a firm verbal and visual overview of the community I served. To reinforce a point made earlier that bears repeating, I learned that newscasts were really only snippets of daily life: accidents, people's reactions to a variety of things, some warning signs, explanations of why this or that happens, indicators of coming events—good & bad, and directions for some common malady or problem. Individually or in tandem, they can wet the tip of a viewer's tongue but not enough to change the world or guide his community through life's challenges. In the next chapter this concept of trying to relate to the community takes on a harder edge through promotion.

As mentioned, there are always those stories that touch our hearts and can even transfix us if the reporter is respectful of his profession and sensitive to his audience. When that happens the feeling at home will rival the excitement in the newsroom…and the community is all that much richer.

I can't remember his name but he was older, over 45, and unsmiling. He was a photographer for CBS news, one of those guys who has seen everything and is impressed and intimidated by nothing. He had been all over the world, seen and filmed significant events of staggering proportions and looked like he could drink turpentine from a paper cup. He also just happened to be the best in his field and I felt I was about to be introduced into a league of students being taught their chosen profession by a consummate master. It would be like learning acting from DeNiro, painting from Picasso or writing from Hemingway. And it was all by example. And to my everlasting shame I don't remember his name.

He had arrived in Salt Lake City on the final few days of a life and death struggle for a miner trapped in a small pocket completely surrounded by rock, dirt and timber. The miner's name was Buck Jones, an employee of a mining company of Lark, Utah, on the far West side of the Salt Lake Valley. Five days before—a full five days before—Buck and five of his fellow miners were deep in one of the veins of the mine. And then, as the song goes, *"there came that rumble way down in the ground."* The men quickly scrambled from what surely be a would-be grave. They ran straight away from the cave-in that soon followed. When they emerged into a secure area, they realized Buck was not among them. They retraced their steps back into the mine but were blocked by the avalanche of debris. Buck was either under the tons of rocks or on the other side, badly injured or, and less likely, had found a safe haven. The latter, everyone felt, was only a dim possibility.

But miners are an intrepid lot. They forge friendships and loyalties that last a lifetime. When one hurts, they all hurt. The nature of their work, together in lighted darkness ten hours a day, creates a single soul of a single thought. Now Buck Jones lay somewhere behind or under the rumble. The remaining five grabbed whatever they could to begin the almost impossible task of going through rock to retrieve Buck, dead or alive. Soon there were joined by a contingent from other parts of the mine.

It was a disaster of substantial scope and the media were quick to respond. It had been a season of soft news but there was an environment of anticipation. Though the news generally had been routine for a number of days, newspaper city editors and radio and television assignment editors were prepared to pounce. And now, here it was, drama right in their valley, on the foothills of the Ocquirrh Mountains where copper was king. There were other metals being taken out but copper had the spotlight for many decades. Buck and his bunch were working in a rarely used but important auxiliary mine near the main artery trying to retrieve what copper was available.

Reporters set up camps with relay teams for relief. National news was, at least for the moment, uninterested. The Mid Western states were used to being ignored on the nightly newscasts unless some catastrophic event took place that shook both coastlines. Buck Jones was small potatoes. To the major networks, the tale of a little man being trapped was not even a bleep on the radar screen. Of course, *if* there had been a cave-in in a sewer line beneath a New York City sidewalk there would be round the clock coverage and even folks in Saco, Montana would have to be observers with the rest of the nation. But in Utah, for the first few days it was just a case of a probable dead Utah miner too slow to out-run the spill.

Once the local media got a glimpse of the magnitude of the cave-in, they too held out little hope. In fact, after three days of digging and no sound from Buck, everyone left, except five tired, dirty, already worn out miners…Buck's comrades-in-arms. They steadfastly refused to leave.

Even the news media generally sticks around until the last whimper by anyone, packed up and joined the other departing miners. I was not unlike the rest of the reporters on the scene. I knew chances were slim-to-none in finding Buck alive, but KSL News had a stringer who had shot film and filed stories for us whenever we were shorthanded, which was about every other day. His name was Al Brain, an overweight, aging, former pharmaceutical drug salesman. He was always, and I mean always, ready to shoot a story and tape record some police officer or on-scene official. And while he didn't investigate a story or do any kind of research, Al was our security blanket for late breaking news before the budget allowed for more people and broadcast toys. He shot both stills and 16mm. He was older than the rest of us and had more of the discipline that comes with maturity and a fascination with the media. It was a combination that we tried to instill in our more youthful reporters and photographers. It was

Al who joined the rest of us at Lark. It was his expectation only to be close to an unfolding story without actually contributing in any way. As it turned out, he was our ace in the hole.

When hope of survival faded and the inevitable seemed certain, we all begin to think of the next big thing. Like most journalists, we were looking for more instant gratification. There were only so many ways you could report a story when there was no progress. It was a shame that we had to leave this father of eleven children buried under rock but it was a profession he had chosen and knew the risks. There was nothing for the rest of us to do. We had kept the drama alive for three days with no end result. Old news is no news and unless there is a compelling reason to stick with a story, there is a hurried exit. The Buck Jones saga had appeared to run its course and all that was left was to close and bull doze the mine. And that's probably what would have happened, except for the loyalty and love of Buck's five fellow miners. It was only our own resolute Al Brain who recorded their continuing effort to free their companion. As the rest of us were leaving town, Al had asked me if he could stay another day and night. He had "a feeling" and wanted to see it through. Frankly, I felt a little better leaving him at the scene. You always feel uneasy about leaving a story without resolution.

News is a mysterious mistress. It traps people into thinking this marvelous service is being performed for the benefit of mankind. Journalists wear the badge of *the "people's right to know"* like some impenetrable shield. It gives them a passport to invade, charge forward, illuminate, investigate, tap into a cell phone or E –mail, challenge comments and promises of public officials and do it all in the name of serving the public and promoting the American way. And maybe, just maybe, along the way, once in a while, something will come from all this dedication that will make it all worthwhile, whether in terms of truly providing information to the viewers that will assist in helping them be more informed…or in some inspirational sense that will lift their spirits and provide heart, hope and haven for the future. The latter was true for the Buck Jones story.

"He's alive." Al Brain's voice in the phone at three in the morning jerked me wide awake in an instant. I told him 'I'm on my way.' On the car's two-way radio he filled me on details that were scanty but enough to know we had a hell of a story on our hands…and for a brief moment were the only ones in town to have it. Sometimes that's all you need to get the front row seat and keep it. A news bulletin on radio took only minutes to alert the rest of the media and for the next three days we camped out in Lark…waiting for the conclusion of this incredible saga.

Literally minutes before Al called me, the five faithful, dedicated, unwavering companions, after moving rock and debris for hours on end, paused just long enough to hear a sound that one described as '*heaven sent*.' Buck was within earshot and could hear the digging and now *they* could hear *him*, barely, but enough to know he was alive and reasonably uninjured. It all happened in fairly rapid succession from that point.

The mine's internal structure was reinforced as much as possible, knowing another cave-in was unthinkable. Still, removal of rock and debris was an agonizingly deliberate process. A tube was slowly forced through the rumble to Buck through which was passed food and vials of water. Miraculously, Buck had reached a small corner clearing, hunkered down and hoped for the best. The best was a very small space, big enough to squat and that was about it, not a place for a claustrophobic.

By the time I reached the scene, Al was feeding live reports to KSL radio's all night talk show and with his tape recorder interviewed a few of the rescuers. He was the center of the universe at three in the morning. He later told me that outside his family, this was his finest moment. Until his death twenty years later, Al proudly wore the mantle of a journalist, if only for a day. He may have been a damn good drug salesmen and a valuable stringer for a TV station on gathering useable film on accidents, etc…but for that **one** shining moment, he was also the best reporter on the planet. It was from Al that the other media had learned of the miracle in Lark and before dawn the small mining town was again jumping with local journalists.

Now that it was established that Buck was alive, CBS finally decided it was worth sending a rookie reporter and prop him up with a seasoned photographer. The networks with their many resources and paraphernalia decided to wait a while before they rolled the dice on a major story   It was estimated it would take another two or three days to retrieve Buck from his dog house sized home for the last five days.

This was Utah and while we had our share of national news over the years, most of it was negative, putting the state in a dim scarlet spotlight. Even the Buck Jones story wasn't pithy enough for the national viewer, at least not yet. So for three days the young CBS reporter dutifully filed his reports and the network anchor would give it a ten second 'read' (with no film). Now if it had been a man trapped under that same New York sidewalk, there would have been around-the-clock coverage.

As the moment edged closer to Buck's release from the mine, the three local stations were second guessing each other as to how the others were going to handle it.   Two of the three were preparing a documentary wrap beginning with the first report of the cave in and ending with the release. I was producing our 'doc' so was more than casually interested in the most dramatic approach to take.

When it was obvious the breakthrough to Buck was just a few hours away I started to enter that twilight zone producers experience when the time and outcome of a story were uncertain.   A hundred questions started to inundate whatever thinking process I had left after seven days and very little sleep… with an added burden to beat the competition with the best coverage on the release of Buck. Would he walk under his own power to the waiting ambulance that had just arrived? That he would go to and stay in the hospital for a spell was certain, but would we be allowed to ask questions as he made his way to the ambulance? Even the officials didn't know. Would he, Buck, even want to answer questions? What would you ask him if questions were allowed, keeping in mind, the obvious. *How else would you feel sitting Indian style for seven days?* Would the media conduct themselves with any kind of dignity or would we be shouting this or that question at poor ole Buck? What was appropriate for our local conduct? Heaven forbid; we didn't want to come off as country bumpkins to the big boys (networks). On the newscast, how much time should be allocated to the rescue, to Buck and his family, to the rescuers, to mine safety, etc. The answer wasn't very far off.

No matter how much imagination is generated with equipment, live shots, special effects and the immediacy of the moment, there are still the determination and passion of the reporter and cinematographer. What they bring to the table in terms of skill, experience and working with human behavior are vital to any story in how to get that "edge" or learning another trick-of-the-trade, among others. My "experience" was about to take a giant leap.

While processing all the options in a mind that was quickly deteriorating, I noticed, leaning on the building, taking long slow drags off a cigarette, was the grizzled old CBS photographer. For the past few days he had pretty much kept to himself. He struck us as a little cantankerous and maybe a little bored with the whole proceedings. For openers he didn't even want to be there. He had just returned to stateside after a foreign assignment and was looking for some time off. It could have been a prominent citizen under the rock pile and he wouldn't have shown more concern or interest. I learned that over the years there was very little these photographers hadn't seen and very few people, kings on down, they hadn't taped and filmed.

So with bloodshot eyes and a lump in my throat I sauntered over to the man with a vacant stare in his eyes and asked how he planned to cover Buck when he was finally being brought out of the mine, which would be within a few hours. He waited about ten seconds before he ventured an answer, dropping his cigarette to the ground and grinding it out with this foot.

"First off, my boy, they will immediately put Buck on a stretcher. Second, he'll answer no questions. He'll only have eyes for that heavy-set lady over there."

Good grief! Buck's wife had arrived on the scene and I didn't even notice her. My youth was failing me at the worst possible time.

"Third," said my newest best friend,*"...the real story is inside the ambulance. Now follow me, son and I'll show you how to handle that part of it."*

I felt like I was in journalism 101 and was following Edward R. Murrow down from the mountain.

The ambulance driver was sitting behind the steering wheel of his vehicle reading, waiting, when my leader approached him. Pulling out a twenty dollar bill from his wallet, he said, *"Here, pal, do me a favor will ya? When Buck is shoved in the back, stall for at least three minutes. Look under your hood and say you've had trouble with a loose wire, anything at all that will buy me some time."* The driver simply said, *"Ok, you've got it."*

With that assurance, my main man got inside the back of the ambulance and taped a microphone to the roof and strung the cable up to the front and outside to where he could plug it in to his camera when the time was right. While I watched a master at work he looked over at me and said…*"Anticipation, my boy, that's the key. Anticipate like it is really going to happen. Now we wait."*

In approximately two hours Buck emerged. He was placed on a stretcher and reached out his hand to the heavy set lady who held it all the way to the parked ambulance...and then…only Buck and his wife got in the back. Buck whispered to the attendant he wanted to ride alone with his wife to the hospital…and of course, Buck's head was directly under the mike. The CBS photographer, as if to say, *I told me so*, winked. His line about the real story being *inside* the ambulance was starting to take shape.

The ambulance sat motionless while the driver was under its hood. My man had been with the rest of the local photographers filming Buck being brought out of the mine from his two by two by three foot high tomb. He followed Buck, as we all did, to the ambulance. And then, unlike the rest, he proceeded to separate himself from the rookies. The ambulance was not the box kind of today but rather looked more like a large station wagon. While the local boys were putting their cameras up to and against the expanse of glass wrapping around the ambulance to film Buck and his wife on the inside—picking up only sounds from the *outside*—my new mentor, who would rather be home, went to his staked out position which just happened to be filled by a young local. He simply said, *"You're standing in my slot."* The man moved. The voice and look of experience then reached down and retrieved the hidden cable end of his microphone and plugged it into his camera. The only sound *he* would be getting was coming from *inside* the ambulance. What he caught on film was astonishing.

Buck and his wife had 11 children and for five days while the rest of the community thought Buck was dead…his wife knew better, with tears in her eyes, saying….

>…Oh, daddy….the kids and I never gave up hope.

Buck: *Oh Mama, you just couldn't image what it was like in there.*

Mrs. Jones: *Oh Daddy, I knew you were going to be ok. Everyone had given up, but I didn't Daddy. I knew you were going to come back to me.*

Buck: *I thought of you every minute and I prayed I would see you and the kids again.*

Mrs. Jones: *Daddy, you're with me and everything is going to be alright.*

And then came the money line that made it all worthwhile. A line you pray for when you stick your mike in someone's face; a line that comes unexpectedly out of the blue; a line that only comes from the anticipation of something incredible happening and being prepared to handle it.

The photographer was the only one who anticipated such a moment. With the camera tight on Buck's face with tears in his eyes as well, he whispered to his loving wife in a breaking voice…

>…Oh mother…I would never have made it if the Lord hadn't had
>his arms around me.

Wow!! And only one man got it. The mere words didn't fully explain the impact of the moment. The look in Buck's face, his tears, and the extraordinary range of emotions obvious in his wife's face, all coupled with Buck's quiet words knocked us out. With those final words the photographer knew he had what he wanted. He literally cut the mike cord from the camera with his pocketknife and gave the high sign to the driver who miraculously found the trouble with his ailing engine and roared off into the night air with Buck, his wife and a CBS microphone.

I asked the photographer how he knew that only Buck and his wife were going to be alone in the back of the ambulance and how, from his vantage point, that his view would be the best to film the two of them and they would say the things they said? He just looked at me and carefully said…*"Remember what I told you? Use your eyes and ears and anticipate it like it's really going to happen. You'll never be disappointed."* With that, he walked away and I never saw him again…but I will never forget him and the lesson he taught me that night in Lark, Utah.

Later, in the station, the news director of a competing station, after seeing our piece on the air, called up and said…"How the hell did you get the sound from the two of them together?" I just said, *"Well, I'll tell you, my boy. It's all in the preparation."* He unkindly told me to stick it where the sun don't shine and hung up.

The next night it ran on CBS News as the final, but dramatic, story. Upon Buck's last words there was no signoff by the reporter…just a slow fade to black and then up to the anchor who could barely say his patented close of the newscast. He just swallowed hard and very quietly signed off.

There was an interesting footnote to the Buck Jones story. We were all at the hospital the next morning to hear the survival story from Buck himself but all we got was a press handout which stated Buck intended to sell his story to the highest bidder. The idea was put in Buck's mind by the hospital administrator. We were shut out from a great follow up to a great story. In the end there were no bidders, high or low, and Buck did eventually go to his grave twenty years later with his story still untold. Six months after Buck was retrieved from the Lark mine he was trapped in another cave-in that put him in the hospital again with greater injuries…and again he lived to see another day.

A footnote to Buck's story amazed us almost as much as his first escape. As a gesture of gratitude to Buck and his wife, the mining company offered to send them *anywhere* in the world for two full weeks with *every* expense paid. They chose Southern Utah.

Formula for success: rise early, work hard, strike oil.
J. Paul Getty

At least Getty was a realist…and probably offers the most realistic piece of advice to those who judge success on how much money you have or make during a career. And if a student is thinking about making a fortune in journalism, fugetaboutit, unless, of course, he/she writes a best seller on a spectacular case. For many, journalism is a just a stopover on life's highway which may be the reason the industry is in such disarray. There are some lifers and that is to a viewer's advantage but there are too many short-timers that get a taste of what its like to contribute to people's knowledge, but then leave to wallow in the taller grass in a neighboring field. As Tucker Carlson states it… *no-one settles in for a long career in TV. It is just the nature of the business. No one is indispensable. There is no one who can't be replaced.* So when you hear a reporter say he is the voice of the people…be wary, be very, very wary. Most haven't earned the right.

Jackie Gleason: *I absolutely love being an actor.*
Interviewer: *What would you do if you couldn't be an actor.*
Jackie Gleason: *I'd shine actors' shoes.*

That kind of devotion to a profession is hard to fine. Still, there are a few journalists out there who truly love the business and never tire of the attention it demands. But, on a local level, that same devotion to duty is elusive.

Of course, as in all professions, there is good and bad news for the journalist. The good news is there is travel, getting ringside seats to just about anything, meeting celebrities, high rollers, community and national leaders, highly interesting and accomplished individuals as well as derelicts who live in a cardboard box under an overpass, and knowing what goes on in the inside of something that most people only see from the outside. The bad news is that maybe a journalist is not such a hotshot after all. It seems anybody with a curious mind and some natural writing ability can be a journalist. No degree, no certificate, no diploma and no membership in anything are required. Even plumbers have to be certified, cops have to go to cop school, embalmers have to pass a test, and doctors have their Hippocratic Oath. Obviously, it would be much better to have a degree but it is not a requirement. There are no shingles on the walls of a newsroom.

It is rightly felt that the basic mechanics of reporting, editing, producing and even anchoring are skills learned more on the job than in a classroom. It's those other urges and yearnings you can't teach. In this business you have to somehow reach way down deep in your gut and find that intangible dimension to your character and personality that will make you a really good reporter or producer. But, it's not as easy as it looks and it's a lot more than writing and responding to an event.

Journalism without a moral position is impossible.
A journalist is a moralist. It's absolutely unavoidable.
A journalist is someone who looks at the world and the way it works,
someone who takes a close look at things everyday and reports what he sees,
someone who represents the world events for others.
He cannot do his work without judging what he sees.

Marquerite Duras

A journalist, moral or not, has to earn his/her title, with or without a degree. He/she has to know the community, its people and problems as well as the physiological and mental restraints that accompany any assignment. The late John Chancellor wrote that *all reporters share a communality of experience. By the very nature of their work, they spend time with the hungry, the poor, the dispossessed, and as a result they develop an attitude toward life, a bias, if you will…a bias toward national solutions to known problems, a bias toward social action, a bias toward people really trying to help, a bias toward pragmatism and common sense.*

Further, reporters have a nasty habit of writing down and remembering what politicians promise and even a nastier practice of reminding them *what* they promised. Reporters walk a narrow path almost everyday. Most, unconsciously, try to follow Benjamin Franklin's advice for a reporter's conduct; *be civil to all, sociable with many, familiar with few, friend to one, an enemy to none.* My friends, it ain't easy.

Let me tell you about our profession.
We are the meanest, nastiest bunch of petty, jealous,
sons a bitches
who ever lived. You think I wouldn't sell my mother for
another My Lai?

Seymour Hersh

Pretty tough stuff! And compared to Ms. Duras' assessment of journalists, somewhat of a conflict…but both Duras' and Hersh would probably find common ground more often than not. A reporter can be a moralist and still be meaner than a snake. A boss once told me, *be angry as much as you want, but be fair and accurate in your story.* I've met a few who fit Hersh's description to a T, but somehow they manage to do the right thing most of the time…which is, or should be, a universal goal for all respectful individual reporters. And most mothers of journalists should feel reasonably assured their offspring will do what is right and not sell out to the highest bidder.

One producer for CBS news, in responding to a question about what guides him in selecting a story for the air, said *his gut is his guide.* One only hopes that his gut is fed and nurtured with years of experience, maturity, responsibility and sensitivity to community needs. And even if all these qualities exist he still has a very narrow window on the world…but even less on an individual community. Eric Severeid once made the comment that all filming of Vietnam war scenes should have been done with a wide angle lens and then the viewer would see the farmer working in his field while a war was being waged on his neighbor's plot of ground. The same is true with just about any situation. Life does go on no matter what people's problems may be or where in the world all hell is breaking loose. Short of having a comet slam into the earth…our lives continue unabated.

In the scheme of things, a local television newscast, in the immortal words of Humphrey Bogart, *doesn't amount to a hill of beans.* A lot of things happen and some get reported, but darn few. The chief complaint by the viewer is not that something was reported inaccurately but that it wasn't reported at all, namely… *'the good things in the community.'* This constant assertion is easily countered. In truth, any given newscast is full of positive stories. It's just that the floods, fires, killings, storms, scandals, human tragedies and accidents have such an overwhelming impact that any of the 'good' is obliterated. Place a murder-suicide story next to an incredible innovation in the medical field—

short of finding a cure for cancer—and see what story surfaces in your mind ten minutes later.

To repeat a point and quote made in the *first terrible truth,* part of the problem is wrestling with the definition of news. Remember what David Brinkley said when defining news... *"News is what I say it is."* …the most profoundly and presumptuous statement made in an industry of presumptuous statements but his experience and maturity carried the day. And of course whenever the network promoted his programs, he was called *experienced, mature, responsible and sensitive*, and for once, we believed it. Ah…promotion. You just hope the promoter is as experienced, skilled and honest as the person(s) he/she is promoting.

It's amazing how we learn lessons in our lives. What might work for one wouldn't affect another in the slightest way. When I was a sophomore in high school my mother got my attention so sharply I will never forget it and still remember it every morning.

We lived in a trailer house in North Richland, Washington when I was thirteen. In fact, it was a trailer town with paved streets, etc., but still no double-wides. They came later. Since mom and my step-dad both worked, it was necessary for everyone to do their part to keep the place clean and picked up. They slept in the bed at one end of the 23-foot trailer and I slept on the couch at the other. I got up at 4:30 every morning to deliver about 75 newspapers (Portland Oregonian) and when I finished I sold another 50 or so at the gates where the men caught buses to go out to the Hanford Atomic Energy Plant.

I then raced home where I made my bed and put everything I was responsible for into its proper place. Mom and Grant had long since gone to work. It was a game of minutes because I then had to walk a block to catch an 8:00 school bus to Richland, another 45 minutes away. It wasn't that I was so responsible with my duties; I just had no other options. I did recognize the work ethic of my parents and the need to hold up my end.

One particular morning I was running late and didn't make up the bed. I thought, quite foolishly, that I would get home in time to make it before anyone else arrived. But in the third period, a vice-principal came to the room and asked that I come to the office. I hurried behind the man who had no answers to anything. In his office sat my mother. She stood when I walked in and said quietly, *"Let's go."* We rode back to North Richland without saying a word, much less the reason for coming to get me.

When we arrived home I followed mom up the single step into the trailer where she pointed at the unmade couch bed and said, "Make it!" and turned to leave. I called out, *"That's it? That's why you got me out of school?"* She said, "Everyone pulls his weight around here" and headed for the car. I said, *"Wait till I make the bed. I need a ride back to school."* She simply said, *"Catch the city bus…"* and proceeded to get in the car and drive off. Today kids could report their parents to the principal and a social worker would report to your home.

I made the bed and had to walk five blocks to catch a city bus back to Richland. Being thirteen years old I felt a little betrayed because I worked my tail off everyday. After school I delivered the Tri-City Herald on another paper route. Dragging me home to make a bed seemed like the punishment didn't fit the crime…so I plotted to get the best of her. A stupid idea as it turned out. I had survived the day and that night nothing, absolutely nothing, was said about the earlier event. But I still shuffled the cards for another round.

The next morning I went through the same ritual with my papers and this time had time to spare to do my chores and catch the school bus but, still trying to get an upper hand, I decided to NOT make the bed again. I was determined to run her to death coming to school to bring me home. The only reason she caught me the day before was that she had forgotten something and made a quick trip home to pick it up…and then saw the unmade couch.

Frankly, I was a nervous wreck all day at school, expecting every second to have a visit from the vice principal. When school was over I was flush with victory stepping on the school bus to go home. I was riding high *until* I approached the trailer and there piled on the small porch was everything I owned in the world, with my bicycle thrown on the top. *The thrill of victory* quickly turned *into the agony of defeat.*

"Mom, what's this about?"
"You know darn well what it's about."

I was to look for another place to live. I learned then and there that my mother was the inventor of that famous game we play everyday in one form or

94

another...*hardball.* Nolan Ryan with his 100 mile an hour fastball was a sissy next to my mom. She knew how to play the game and how to win.

With tears in my eyes I tried picking up my stuff without a clue as to where I would take it. She caught me at the end of the walk and said quietly, *"You wanna try it one more time?"* I blubbered a quiet "yes"...and she helped me put my stuff away. Never, ever since that day have I ever left my home with an unmade bed. Never! Now, I have it down to a science. If there was an Olympic medal in bed making, I would get the gold, every year, without question.

My mom is getting rapped pretty bad in this story and before I go any further it must be said that she was a gracious, loving and patient parent, a fine example and the hardest worker this side of the Yangtze. But when she said something, you could take it to the bank. She never went back on her word and she took everything at face value. You didn't play any role with her. Mom could spot a phony ten blocks away. And rules of the house, even if the house was only 225 square feet, were chiseled in granite. Break one and the world stops for a minute until some restitution was complete. But I thought I was an exception. Besides learning bed making and its importance I also learned that with life comes responsibility, however meager the reward. In journalism, reporters, producers, editors and anchors have a responsibility to the viewers and readers. You don't take the easy way out. You make the bed on every story, every day. It's just too bad that the viewers can't chase you down and drag you back to finish the job. It's something they'll have to work on in the future.

Seems everyone has something to say about television news but only a few really know what they're talking about, one of which is The Project for Excellence in Journalism, funded by the Pew Charitable Trusts. Without belaboring their information and not boring you to death, only the basic stuff will be presented.

> ➤ There is a continuing decline in the numbers of people watching the early evening news, except there are indications that the late local news is improving its numbers.
> ➤ Of all the local media, TV news stories emerge as the most thinly sourced and shallowly (their words) reported of any medium studied other than local radio.

Roughly half of all the news on local TV news that was not given over to weather, traffic and sports was devoted to crime and accidents. Stories about local institutions, government, infrastructure, education and more were generally relegated to brief anchor reads in the middle of the newscast.

> There are two views of local TV news;
>> A. …that local TV news is down to earth, deals with topics that are community-based and is aimed at what regular people care about.
>> B…that local TV news is the same everywhere and that it is all about mayhem and emotion, punctuated by traffic and weather.

Extensive research found that there is just enough truth in both A&B that the two sides keep on arguing. Four traits stand out:

- …viewers get a lot of local weather, traffic and crime. As for other news, there were usually just three or four items received anything more than a brief anchor report.
- …local TV news is more likely than other media to try to portray regular people from the community and how they feel about things.
- …the reporting was straightforward and mostly strictly factual.
- …as local newsrooms are stretched thinner by producing more hours, anchor reads without correspondents are increasingly more important. Reporters are saved for those stories that are believed to be audience grabbers with the anchors to handle the bulk of stories about such matters as budgets, government, infrastructure and civic institutions. The brevity of the coverage, in turn, creates a cycle in which viewers look elsewhere for coverage with some authority.

> TV news spends twice as much time on crime and accidents than daily newspaper coverage. Crime and accidents also dominated all three time slots 47 % of morning news time,52% of early evening and 50% late night. Even though morning news is slipping it is mostly the source for what happened the night before followed by traffic and weather.

➢ In the study of early evening and late night news, a distinctive pattern emerges. These newscasts demonstrated what has come to be called the *"hook and hold"* approach to local TV news. The phrase refers to the habit of opening the newscast with visuals that are meant to be alarming and eye grabbing—flashing red lights and yellow police tape—to get to the broadcast's lead story, then repeatedly teasing viewers with the promise of another report, held till the end to try and keep people from changing channels.

➢ The decline in viewers for the early evening newscast is seen as coming from increasing pressure from changing lifestyles, longer commutes and greater competition for people's time from everything from homework to iPods to more channels on the TV dial.   Fewer people are at home this early anymore but instead are still at the office or facing longer commutes.

➢ The late news is better fit with people's schedules today, which also speaks to the better numbers for late news.

➢ Unlike later newscasts, morning newscasts, morning news is presented quickly and succinctly, and repeated often so viewers can dip in and leave.

The Project for Excellence in Journalism

5.

You cannot judge a Television news operation by its promotion.

We want to bring you information accurately, fairly.
And we want to hold the people in power
accountable for their words and their actions.
                                        Anderson Cooper
                                        CNN

This statement by Cooper, or by the CNN promotion department, is probably the most insightful promotional line a journalist—print or electronic—could use in either promoting or defining his/her profession. It describes what a station/ reporter is trying to do on a daily basis and at the same time defines the higher road of the journalism industry. There is nothing complicated about it and why this simple premise somehow gets lost in the shuffle by journalists, viewers and readers alike, is one of life's little mysteries. Granted, the journalism industry and how it works is more complicated than a couple of sentences. The trouble arises when reporters fail to do their jobs on behalf of the viewers or when viewers fail to hold the reporters accountable for the information they present or when both get lazy and shortchange themselves and their community. But that's why there's advertising and marketing: to remind the viewers how skilled a particular station's news department is…and to remind the reporters *who* they are and *what* they are suppose to be doing. Sometimes it works.

The real fun and games in the business of news begin when the promotion and marketing department starts fishing around to find ways to best promote the station's news department. One would hope they would actually spend time *in* the newsroom soaking up as much information as possible and then—drawing on the philosophy and strength of the news director, producers, reporters and editors—to come up with an original line or campaign that would describe the difference between them and the other guys. But then that would be too obvious and time consuming. Invariably, they find other easier and more subtle ways to put their station on the map.

Sadly, there really isn't much difference between you guys, those guys and the other guys. The distinction is generally in the anchors and we'll talk about that at length. All the stations are trying to do the same thing: grab the biggest share of the viewers, cover stories that would hold viewer interest and possibly give them a leg up on life. Being clever and edgy is always a plus…but mostly, make management happy and money for the station. They're no different than competing banks that do the same thing with their matching interest rates, friendly tellers, smiling managers and keeping an eye on the bottom line. The difference, like the TV stations, is in the advertising. And frankly, what works for one bank would be just as effective and just as believable if the same campaign was used for its arch rival.

The fact is most good promotional lines are interchangeable from one station to another. It's just who lands on it first…and frankly, much of the really good or clever promotional lines are syndicated. Travel around the country and you'll see promotional clones of your local TV news operations. None of this is to say that news departments are less than what are advertised. Even with all their faults, the Salt Lake City market, for instance, has four of the finest TV News presentations in the country. But in each one, there is a disparity in the effort and philosophy between the news operations and the promotion. Of the former, there is the daily grind to determine what is happening in their coverage area, striving to be first on the scene, making decisions on how this or that is going to be covered, trying to represent all stories with honestly and being as creative as possible; and the latter, *whatever* will work to sell a newscast…even *if* the promotion director is playing footsie with the truth to bring in an extra viewer or two.

Good consistent promotion can lift a station in the ratings. It doesn't have to be fair or even very accurate. Just clever and consistent. I know one station that saw an infinitesimally small increase with the line, *We're earning our reputation.* They followed it with *news people you can trust.* When voiced as a promotion the announcer is tactfully saying the reporters and producers of the other stations are *un*trustworthy. Another station in the same market promoted itself as being the '*source of news.'* The other stations, it is saying, are dealing in second hand information for their newscasts. The third station calls its reporters *the news specialists.* Of course, the implication here—like the others, with the tongue firmly planted in it's cheek—is that the other stations have reporters who are arbitrary in their coverage, not having reporters who are properly familiar with the topics they cover, with the added allusion that there are too many young bucks out there without experience and maturity. Even the most naïve viewer knows all this promotion is just plain hype and doesn't mean a whole lot.

If the viewer watches closely he/she will see that reporters jump from one station to another as much as bees flit from one flower to another. So a reporter may be a '*news specialist'* at one station and suddenly becomes a *'news person you can trust'* at another. I know one anchor man who worked at three of the four major stations in Salt Lake City so, over time, could lay claim to several different titles, none of which really mean a damn thing.

COVERS DIXIE LIKE THE DEW
Slogan of the Atlanta Journal Constitution

Now there is a slogan. You can almost see it and feel it. Short and crisp, faithful to the region, non-pretentious, non-offensive, a simple fact of life, relatable, light hearted but serious, visible in your mind's eye, beautifully descriptive and rolls nicely off the tongue.

And then there is a local bank with the tag line*: We Haven't Forgotten Who Keeps Us In Business.* And that means what exactly? It could be used by any bank in the galaxy. At least Wal-Mart's *Save Money, Live Better* has meaning and moxey. But what does "forgotten" mean? The bank certainly isn't going to do anything out of courtesy; it is in business to make a buck and with late fees, overdrafts, interest rates, service fees and a dozen other charges, etc. the customer is certainly doing all he/she can to keep the bank in business.

Only occasionally do you hear a slogan for a TV news operation that lingers in a viewer's mind. There aren't a lot of *Dixie Dews* out there. The fact is, most TV news operations have no control over their promotion and some don't like how they are being promoted. They want to be journalists and not public relations specialists. Putting together a TV newscast is a remarkable task, fraught with deadlines, long hard hours and pressures from within and without. Trying to marry everyone's work into a single entity, and do it well, takes an enormous amount of skill.

For all the terrible truths about local TV newscasts, there is an amazing effort going on that people don't see but would greatly appreciate if they could be a mouse in the corner. Everyone at all channels generally earn their wings not through promotional channels but with gritty, day to day, busting their butt type of reporting and producing. Never mind that much of what they put out is crap...so in a lot of ways, it is energy wasted, but still admirable in the effort.

Admittedly, companies of all stripes, along with their advertising & marketing agencies, are in love with slogans...and print and electronic entities are no different. Some slogans have been so successful, they have become a part of our language. In a few words they can tell a whole story, define a philosophy or establish a trust...and companies pay fortunes for them. People still sing the old McDonald's "You Deserve a Break Today." Maxwell House Coffee's "Good to the Last Drop" will never die in the minds of anyone over sixty. (Ironically, it was President Theodore Roosevelt who coined the phrase.)

Some slogans challenge the imagination, some are hypocritical, some don't make sense and some are just outright stupid...but they are never going to leave our advertising landscape as long as there is at least one company left standing. And when the wrecking ball swings for the last time, it will be the company's defining statement lying proudly on top of the rubble. The New York Times has had the same motto for well over a hundred years--*All the News that's Fit to Print.* In fact, most papers keep their signature line for years, never to change them. Some have tried but eventually revert to the one that brought them to the dance. Local TV news operations, on the other hand, seem to change their motto at the start of every new campaign push, thankfully. Because the standard line about a station's news operation is repeated so often, it eventually loses its meaning and impact.

Promotional lines are a necessary evil viewers have to face. On a single nightly newscast, one isn't surprised to hear the slogan or some version of it, a half dozen times, plus, they have to endure it during the rest of the day on scheduled promotional spots. One station used the term "Fresh Air" in its promotion of news, weather and sports. I guess it means that all their stuff is "fresh." Or does it mean they never repeat anything about any story they previously aired? Who knows? Who cares?

ABC says, "Because It Matters Where You Get Your News,"… as opposed from getting it from your brother-in-law who works in a furniture store and doesn't have a clue as to what is going on.

CBS News used a single word, "Experience." It's simple and I'm sure they used focus groups and spent a million bucks testing it.

At one point NBC used a stylized "N" as a logo…but then was sued by the Nebraska Public Broadcasting network because it used a similar "N" as its identifying symbol. NBC's John Chancellor, in reporting the story, said the Nebraska facility spent $150 on its "N" … and NBC spent… (long pause)… *more*. One can only imagine. At least it is refreshing to know that once in a great while a network can make fun of itself.

Probably the most successful and most consistent name given to a newscast is "Eyewitness News." It worn very well over the years, mainly because it doesn't insult your intelligence and, without blowing their bugle every ten minutes, the message is implicit; the station saw it happen and wants to share the experience. But then they followed it up with a tag line that makes no sense at all…"Your News!" "Eyewitness" says it all. "Your News" means it belongs to us? In what way? Or is it about us? Just what does ownership mean? Is it about the stuff we care about or think about or hate or wish we were apart of, or does it mean the only news covered is what I like, enjoy, or want to know about? "The line sucks," one anchor told me. The station eventually dropped the "Eyewitness News" identity and went with "The News Specialists." Enuf said already.

One campaign staged by a local station was so pervasive with its identifying news logo that the station's promotion department had to build a promotional spot to promote the promotional connection. The line, simple in text but questionable in use, is "Close to Home."   While watching the Academy Awards one evening the station gave an ID with the news slogan, "Close To Home," prompting the ten-year-old son of my friend to ask, *"What does that mean?"* The father said, *"I was hoping you knew."* The short answer is…it means *nothing* in terms of the news parameters the station has laid out nor does it describe the news department's uniqueness or the extent of its coverage. A viewer can't discern any on-air change except the exasperating use of the term, "Close To Home."

If a station's news department is just covering news "Close To Home," one wonders whether it even cares about the rest of the state, region, country, etc. To compound the problem, an opposing network had a drama every week called —you guessed it—"Close to Home."

I can hear the conversation in the station's promotion department, slapping each other on the back because not only do I "*not* get it" but I am taking the time to write about it. They're probably quoting that line about the politician who says, *I don't care what the paper says about me; I just want my name spelled correctly.*

Somewhat confused, I called the station itself and asked what was meant by "Close to Home." The answer was…*news that was important to me*. Well, now I know and I'm really impressed how they know what is important to me. How nice. If I have to take the time to determine what a slogan means, I'll ride another horse. Truthfully…while I think the slogan is a stretch, I like the station because I respect the anchors and reporters. They are proficient, pleasing to watch and seemingly professional in most ways. All appear to be competent enough to stray *far from home* and still represent their station and viewers well.

What happens in Vegas, stays in Vegas!
Las Vegas Promotional Theme

Wink, wink. Not only is the Vegas thing a slap at morality but is, in fact, inaccurate. At best, promotion is a tricky business. A station has to promote what it has that is so great. And most promotion, no matter how silly or pompous or irritating, does have some effect. If someone says something enough times even the station will start to believe it. And of course if there *is* a bump in the ratings, the promotion director will get all tingly inside, forgetting just *why* a viewer watches in the first place. The news staff would like to believe people watch because they produce the most comprehensive and professional newscast in town.

However, it's more complicated than that. A line like "close to home" plays a pitifully small role in the success of the station. The way an anchor reads a story, or combs his hair or wears his/her clothes have more clout then some juiced up promotional tag line. Success is dependent on several things: the market, the news anchor, even the weather or sports anchors, and the graphics. All play a role.

Promotion is a necessary evil and may only barely describe the true nature of the news department. An anchor may decide to read the news in the nude, in which case you wouldn't need a promotion department. The fact that it is being done at all would quickly spread but will only last until the viewers feel they've had enough, depending on the anchor of course. At the same time, great anchors, solid news coverage, obvious responsibility to the community, with some courage and discipline thrown in…will go a long way on its own. Promotion would be icing on the cake. Still, you have to remind the folks what you've got and why it is important to them. And then there are those times when you haven't got as much as the other guys but still put out a competent product and the promotion department still has to try to come up with something to make people at least give you a try. The news itself may be lacking but there are still a few reasons for viewers to stick around.

In Atlanta, the anchor of the leading station changes her hairdo so often it has become a topic of conversation among the viewers. The fact that she is also a competent, award winning journalist and has survived a couple of bouts with cancer certainly add to her mystique but those changing hairdos seem to mesmerize a handsome share of the viewers. In the promotion department the phrase "whatever works," is the guiding philosophy. In the newsroom, the journalists hope that gathering the news and informing the good people in Georgia has as much influence as a stylish French cut. It must also be said that no matter how attractive, popular or proficient the anchor, the news product still has to be well covered, expertly produced, and professionally handled on every level… because if it isn't, those hairdos will go to waste. But all things being equal among all the competing stations, that hairdo can be a gold mine in the ratings game.

People will go to see movies that critics lambaste because they like the star. They didn't pay Tom Cruise twenty million dollars a picture because he is such a great actor. He has that X quality that people like and would probably like to see in themselves, as long as they don't get arrested from some despicable crime or jump up and down on Oprah's couch. But even Tom can wear too thin with viewers over time. Staying power only lasts so long.

Even if the station buys every available piece of technology to enhance a newscast, people will not necessarily watch because the picture is going to twirl around like a twelve year old ballerina or provide a three dimensional look at some one reading of the state's budget. Some watch—in fact, quite a sizeable chunk watch—because they like the anchorman or woman. And that's why anchors make the big bucks just reading someone else's copy and/or introducing reporters in the field who may be standing in a blizzard waiting for their cue. Anchors are being paid three times or more than the guy in the blizzard, because the viewer likes them, trusts them, gets all gooey over their voice or face, admires their clothing, or the way they comb their hair. It has nothing to do with technology or because the station was first on the scene or has exclusivity on a story. In the viewer's mind the anchor of a newscast is being invited into their home to tell them what happened in the world that particular day. If they don't feel comfortable with someone, they won't watch, no matter how *close to home* they may be. So when the promotion department gets out the camera, guess who puts their best face forward? A clue: it's not the guy standing in the blizzard.

A news operation in the Salt Lake City market that once lead the market came up with a series of promotional ads that more directly tied the personalities to the viewer, hyping community involvement. The promotion featured each anchor talking a little about themselves and their commitment to news and community, etc. Three cameras were used simultaneously to capture different angles of the individual…and all three views were put in sync and flashed on the screen at the same time. This cute production gimmick, frankly, took away from what each was trying to say, namely…

Anchor: *I think everybody probably has been an underdog at some point where you feel like you just don't have the information, you don't have the power, and you don't have the access. That's sort of our role, I think. We did a story once on Hispanic workers. They were working hard, 12-14 hours a day and their bosses were taking advantage of that. It affects us…if people are taking advantage of your mother, your cousin, your relatives, your friends. That's part of what some of our broadcasting is all about …is helping the people that need a voice.*

What a noble thing to say. And sometimes they even believe it. They make it sound like the news staff will be the big brother they never had, the life-size, strong, rich, smart, big brother who will protect them at whatever cost. Frankly, the best the Hispanic or Caucasian or Black or Oriental or Indian can hope for is a crumb or two every now and then. But, gee, does it ever sound good as a promo. Since the station already had the audience in hand, each promotion was lecturing to the converted. …*helping the people that need a voice?* Nice thought, wrong profession. Informing them, describing something to help bring more understanding, eliminating confusion, featuring an individual's plight, even relating to people's problems…all are part of what a newscast should represent to the community. But being *a voice* for the people is a stretch and a heavy responsibility for a reporter who probably has enough problems of his own. This is a rather presumptuous line for a journalist, even by the many definitions floating around his profession. But sympathizing with viewers, giving them information to help them move to the next step is not the same as being their voice. I know it's a fine line but to put one more toe *over* that line is not within guidelines of the journalistic industry. Some problems can be addressed by taking an editorial stance, but that is not part of a newscast where neutrality is an absolute must.

If the station is so anxious to be an advocate for the viewers, reporters should examine some of the practices by various corporations, mortgage companies, credit card companies and banks who charge customers and clients for those ongoing and never ending charges for which no one seems to have an explanation. Granted, most are legal, but if more people know the whys and wherefores of some of these practices there might be a clamoring to change laws…or at least be able to know what questions to ask. Trust me; as long as questions aren't asked and people stay in the dark about various practices, nothing will change. It will only get worse as it has been doing for the past decade. As long as some industry can get away with some maddening practice that is to their advantage, it will continue on its merry way. So, again, if a news department really wants to be a *voice* or an *advocate* and live up to its promotion, there are many roads to take…but don't expect a rush to the starting gate. And if an offending company happens to be spending a fortune advertising on television, forget about any conclusive investigations. Stations have no teeth when it comes to biting the hand that feeds them, no matter how egregious the offense.

There is one grand exception to this idea of not being a voice for a viewer. There is, in many of the local stations across the country, a reporter known as—(not the *voice* of the consumer)—a consumer advocate. It's generally one consumer being upset with one company. The advocate (or consumer reporter) devotes his or her time to distinguish between the good and bad buys, the efficacy of some products, the unfairness of a company or just responding to a consumer's complaint. In Utah there was a consumer advocate who was one of the best in the nation. *"Get Gebhardt"* went to great lengths to protect individual consumers, getting their money back or getting to the bottom of shoddy practices while holding a company's nose to the fine print in a contact. There was rarely a complaint he couldn't handle. When his station briefly overtook as the lead news operation in the market in a scramble for ratings, much of the credit was put on Bill Gebhardt's shoulders. As far as presenting hard news or following running controversies or explaining the political or community issues of the day, Mr. Gebhardt stuck to his arena of handling individual complaints. He may not have been a voice for overall community concern, but he was a knight in shining armor for people who become victims.

The reporter's authoritative manner and no nonsense approach to get to the root of a problem served him and his station well. Together they stood up for the consumer and against the company that has no pride in their workmanship, morality in their profession or sense of fairness in customer relations. A Bill Gebhart would be an impressive addition to any newscast. Eventually this Gebhart moved on but his son with the same dedication and bravado has taken the reigns and the station now waits for results like those of the father.

The basic reasoning behind all the spots in a promotional series is to make the anchors and the whole news department feel more connected to the community and make the viewers feel the station is looking out for their welfare. And they try and do this by—so states the promotion department—developing stories that reach out and help folks better survive their day *or* give them information how to raise their kids more successfully *or* demonstrate what may be new on the market to make their life better *or* warn them of pitfalls to avoid in their daily journeys, etc. They make it sound like this is a daily commitment to their viewers in trying to connect with the community.

The fly in the ointment in all this promotional horn blowing is when comparing the number of newscasts every day to the number of stories that can truly make a difference in the viewers' lives, it is hardly worth the effort. Only occasionally are the stories done with a comprehension that will actually help someone, even if viewers actually *have time* to sit down and pay attention to them.

The larger concern is that the news department doesn't always air these stories during the prime time newscasts. They are likely scheduled earlier in the day when the audience is about half the size of the late night newscast. By then the producers would rather be awash in blood and guts, tears and fears, controversy, the unusual, politics and personalities rather than all the stuff the promotion department is talking about. When a story of significance *is* produced, it is sometimes watered down to a level of losing its clout or reason to be aired in the first place. The rhythm and reason for the story was effectively established in the original airing. To cut the guts out of it and give it a token airing later does nothing for the subject at hand or the quality of the newscast.

In case you've forgotten, I'll go over it again…it's about flashing red lights, body counts, screw ups, crashes and the rest that build the audience, increase the ratings, bring in money and puts smiles on managements' faces. It is not brain surgery!

A journalist is basically a chronicler—not an interpreter of events
PBS

This distinction is generally lost on the public. Reporters do try to take the confusion out of the many issues facing the public on a daily basis and this is sometimes called interpretation. But between us friends, journalists do a lot of interpretation but call it news. The major dilemma here is that a TV news operation wants to be all things to all people. A newscast barely has enough time to report the nuts and bolts of the day as it is.

There is nothing that says you have to be an advocate for anyone and on a daily newscast it would be an added responsibility. As mentioned, there *is* advocacy journalism that is an acceptable form but it is hardly being a voice for a viewer. That's why there are local talk shows and public service announcements. On occasion, if there is a problem in the community—sometimes unnoticed by a majority of the population—that is addressed in an aggressive reporting style and that is how advocacy journalism is defined. The story takes a position and defends it, forgetting about bringing balance and the flip side of the coin. As mentioned in the first *Terrible Truth,* it is one of several kinds of journalism a viewer is likely to encounter on a local newscast. It also takes skill because it borders on being editorial and being in danger of offending some viewers and innocent commercial companies. Most stations don't have the courage to do a lot of advocacy journalism.   In the 1950's when TV News was becoming a minor force in the industry each station had all it could do to deal almost exclusively in *straight* reporting.

As TV news evolved over the next half century, electronic journalism changed formats, colors, genders, styles, urgencies and subject material. Watch any newscast and you are likely to see two or three styles, or maybe the whole gambit. On a given night a station might air;
>an accident that killed a person and injured three—*straight reporting*;
>a story of a local industry nightly dumping waste into canal water—*investigative reporting*;
>a report on a local sports hero headed for the Olympics—*feature reporting*;
>a twenty year old eye sore that most people would like to see removed—*advocacy reporting*;

110

the TV station pleading the case for speed reduction in the downtown area—*editorial*;
the high local official caught frolicking with a local lady of the night—*tabloid*.

It is this latter form that is gaining the most attention, mainly because it is the most titillating. Your mind gets a workout trying to visualize what took place. Increasingly, tabloid journalism is edging its way into the main stream media. People have shown they have a thirst for it…and ownership of magazines, newspapers, radio and television stations are only too happy to cater to their prurient tastes. Among the last holdouts, television news is slowly lacing their newscasts with spicier stories. If management *didn't* see a corresponding bump in the ratings and a matching boost in revenue, they would quickly say it was *beneath them to air such trash.*

In the same series of promotional spots just mentioned, another anchor said…

> *"Education in this state; our hope is that we have information and a message to you that is relevant to you.   I mean, it's a given that the student population will rise.   Children have to be educated if they're going to compete and have a life style anything comparable to the life style you had. So how are you going to work that out?   I can't decide that for you as a newscaster, but I have the responsibility to give you the information and the pieces so you can decide.   It's your decision and that's why **it's your news.**"*

Mash potatoes, gravy and cranberry sauce! Whoooooooeeeeee!!

As a promotional spot, this takes the pomposity award of the year. It goes way beyond the idea of giving people information about problems or observations in their neighborhood or the world at large. There is a difference between furnishing information to viewers and being a family counselor armed with 'pieces' of data to make a decision on some kid's education. This spot is not only pretentious and presumptuous, but is also a journalistic fairy tale. Giving out *pieces* of information so others can use it to make major decisions? Just where do those "pieces" of information come from? And is the station really capable of providing *enough* "pieces" to make a critical decision? And if the viewer used a minimum of effort he could probably find out the same information from a phone call. Additionally, the chances of a station actually following up on getting more "pieces" on the same subject and putting them in some kind of order is ludicrous. I know that the purpose of the spot is to show how the station is involved with its community. They just picked a lousy and questionable example of doing it. And as sincere as the station is trying to be, the anchor had to close it off with a cheesy news department tag line; *"Its your decision and that's why it's **your news**."*

What works for one family wouldn't fly for another. Both reporters and viewers have to show a great deal of discipline in the information they receive and provide. If the viewer is looking at a television newscast to assist in major decisions in his family, he had better tread carefully in gathering the *bits and pieces* that come his way…and the newscaster had better be careful when presenting information that may be a critical component in a viewer's memory bank. At best, journalists provide information, and if it can be used by the viewers in making a choice, a judgment or an evaluation, so be it. Promotion departments should take heed. And keep in mind the words of Eric Severeid who reminded us that… *the major cause of problems…are solutions.*

There are also some promotional spots being aired where part of a newscast is staged, but passed off as part of an *actual* newscast. It shows the anchor from a couple of different angles talking about a story being used as a promotion but he is using copy that was created specifically for the promotion, not copy that was actually aired, making it sound that the station was going to *"follow up on the story in the days and weeks to come."* (If they actually said that line in an evening newscast once a year, I'd be very surprised.) It's one thing to build a promotional spot and even interview the anchors or reporters for their personal feelings…but to phony up a newscast with dummy copy to make it sound like it was actually aired, smacks at the station's integrity and chokes the life out of the promotional department's credibility.

In the meantime, there are other infringements that are pawned off as journalism but are not fully embraced by working reporters, even though they all are susceptible and not above it if the interest in the story is running high. The most obvious one is *ambush journalism* where the victim is generally an official—national, state or local—or some corporate officer who has done something or is suspected of having done something and is caught off-guard by a reporter and cameraman. It is a little like, in fact, it is *a lot* like the paparazzi. Even though the victim doesn't answer a question, the reporter loves using the video of an embarrassed subject running for the hills. Only rarely will the victim even answer a question. It's no wonder people-on-the-edge don't trust journalists.

Another form of journalism is the increasing use of *caught on film/tape*, a term that has become more and more a part of the industry's attempt to paint pictures with a broader brush stroke. Sometimes a story is already in progress, but other times the story begins at the moment video is supplied to the police departments or some TV news department. It is generally shot by some amateur who collects a handsome paycheck and a reporter that has to walk on egg shells piecing the story together. The incidence of video cameras these days is everywhere. I mean *everywhere*. No one is safe from these ubiquitous intrusions into our lives. There is an old saying that seeing and believing is often wrong…and increasingly, reporters, law enforcement officers and attorneys are finding this to be true.

Caught on tape is an area of journalism that belongs exclusively to television. It transcends every description ever conjured up for *journalism 101*. Dictionaries have to be re-written, exhumation should begin on Ed Murrow and Horace Greeley…and journalism schools need to change their curriculum.

Truthfully, *Caught on Tape* is a little bit of each of 5 major journalism categories we've discussed; hard news, feature, investigative, advocacy and tabloid. It is also the kind of 'journalism' that brings out the voyeur in all of us. It has a particularly firm grip on reporters. Oh, they'll deny it to the grave but in their heart of hearts they know better. It is also where the controversy rages on in the charge of TV news being more show biz than journalism.

To be sure, there is more glitz in a newscast than is probably necessary. From the newscast opening, with music and especially the eye popping graphics, we find the roots of electronic journalism have more than just a little bit of the glittering blood of *show biz* flowing in its veins. And frankly, that's not always such a bad thing. The *caught on tape* craze has a particular appeal on both sides of the fence.

Rodney King, being beaten senseless by police after a traffic stop, was caught on tape by a man in his front yard across the street from where the beating was taking place, and is a conspicuous example of the *caught on tape* brand of reporting. But more and more there are frivolous examples of people being

113

caught doing any number of things. 80% of the people now carry a video camera on their person, so rarely does some dramatic event or anomaly happen without someone getting tape of it. TV stations can download it and have it on the next newscast. The definition of journalism is taking a hit as everyone can participate in at least of part of it.

For example, Matt Lauer, of NBC's Today program once aired video of a three-year-old child standing by the family car with the trunk open. He was playing with a pistol while his parents were 50 yards away drinking a beer and looking at a shooting target. It was taped by a neighbor and sent to NBC news. The average viewer was repulsed by the tape and outraged by what was seen. The next day Lauer interviewed the unrepentant parents who just happen to be gun freaks. Their story, while still a matter of concern, cast a different light on what was seen and believed. Their guns, they said, are never loaded while in the home or car. They are very strict about this practice because of their children. Being gun advocates they take their guns more seriously than casual gun users. And the 'gun' the child was handling just happened to be a toy gun and was aiming at a tree. The parents did not apologize for their actions and said the neighbor who took the video only showed 30 seconds of the 30 minutes of tape that had been shot that showed them taking precautions. Again, there is still concern about the whole incident but it was nothing like the first blush of video exposed to several million people the day before. Seeing and believing sometimes takes more investigation and, frankly, reporter responsibility. No one said being a reporter was a walk in the park.

Caught on tape in March 2005, a five year old Florida girl threw a tantrum in a school, acting as a one-man wrecking crew, taking a room apart piece by piece, breaking everything in sight and vigorously fighting the school administrator. The police were called in to bring calm to the scene. A videotape was made of the last part of her tantrum before police stopped and handcuffed her. When the tape was released a few weeks later all hell broke loose that dominated the news every day for a week or better.

Mothers and fathers were taking sides, lawyers were working at fever pitch, law suits were being discussed, newspaper columnists were writing and TV stations were running the video ad nausea. And all because it was *caught on tape*. Never mind, as columnist Leonard Pitts Jr. pointed out, that in the previous year in St. Louis a kindergartner was handcuffed for disruptive behavior. And in April 2005, a 7 year old in Bethlehem, W. Va., wound up wearing "jailhouse bracelets" for much the same reason. Unfortunately or fortunately the video camera wasn't rolling at the time. A shame, TV news types were deprived of their lead stories and filler video for the next week or so.

The impact of catching something happening on tape is astonishing. It can cause good people to be fired, discover bad people getting away with murder, be the lynchpin at a trial, create incredible controversy, be the difference between time in jail and complete freedom, challenge a culture or create the elements of a sensational news story that would normally die a fast death. Once reserved for the tabloids, *caught-on-tape*/film now ranks as an indispensable ingredient in the evening news. With the proliferation of videotape, cell phones with cameras, and mini cameras the size of a fountain pen are anywhere where something is happening, in or outside a building.

The *caught-on-tape* craze in this modern technological age is now a lot more than an occasional novelty. It is a continuing reality and one that will be a part of the journalistic landscape. And it will also be a subject of controversy, of bitter disagreements, of shock value, of public fascination, of moral decisions… and could ultimately be a stain on the practices revered by first rate journalists. For all reporters, producers and viewers, fasten your seatbelts. Like Bette Davis once told us…"*It's going to be a bumpy ride.*"

The previous information is one of the reasons specific promotion of a news operation is so difficult and why the promotion is so general in nature. Less difficult is to use general terms and words like *trust, professional, committed, concerned, caring, experience, exclusive, dedicated, truth* and *eyewitness* and any other word that is interchangeable with the other stations.

There are other words you never hear in a news promotion but are prevalent with critics and a wary public; *inaccurate, false impressions, guess work, unaccountable, rumor, wrong, double standard, sexy, lazy*—all words that haunt a newsroom. The business is not an exact science. Interestingly, you never see a promotion that publicizes how proficient the news departments are in covering the crime and accidents that eat up 50% of every newscast, complete with spectacular video, sound bites from the police and excited eyewitnesses, even though these stories lead almost every newscast…but are piranhas to every promotion director.

Being a celebrity has its perks but being raw meat to tabloid journalists is not one of them. It is one of life's little ironies that people who are well known for whatever reason are prey to that type of journalism that lays waste to good taste, good manners, respect for privacy and common decency. Journalists who fall into this category can make life a living hell for people. This is hardly a news flash. Regrettably, this lamentable custom isn't going away, no matter how many people rail against it or deplore the practice.

There is another side to that coin that can go too far in the opposite direction. The news can be so soft that individuals who probably should be locked up are given the benefit of the doubt, overlooking all negatives and are asked only softball questions. Being too timid or too apathetic can have a worse effect than being too tough. Even the average viewer with no malice in his/her heart wants an edge to the news. This is the same edge that also makes them vulnerable to all the trashy news.

Strangely, most bona fide celebrities have learned to live their lives with a camera lens in their faces and all their peccadilloes announced on television, but the real tragedy lies with those poor souls who are unheralded celebrities, celebrities because they present a particular skill or have an abundance of courage…and display both at critical times. These people are revered in and out of their profession and are only in the news from time to time because of something that relates to their line of work. They are not exactly celebrities but do have a local connection with the community more than most. Frankly, it is a status in which they personally can take pleasure and their families can enjoy.

But there is a downside that, thankfully, only a few get a chance to experience. If someone is well known and has led an exemplary life, whether the person likes it or not, that life is always a blip on the journalist's radar screen. And if that blip suddenly takes an unexpected turn, it becomes a subject of intense concern to those who have been exposed to that career. The blip suddenly casts a shadow that can't be ignored. It is a time when even a journalist might hate his job but due to the nature of the business—that of reporting news of interest to the people—it *has* to be reported, particularly if the shift touches upon one of society's forbidden taboos.

Most of us go about our business making stupid mistakes and doing irrational or even immoral things and no one outside the family seems to care. But if you or I have a "status" within our profession that has received public attention from time to time, those little "mistakes" in our lives suddenly become everyone's business, thanks to the media and whatever Gods its members worship. And of course, the bigger the mistake the bigger the news.

Journalists say they don't make judgments, they just report the truth and let the chips fall where they may. And of course the more they dig the more sensational the story. Depending upon the depth of the celebrity status and how spectacular the event, that so-called digging goes way beyond the mere surface specifics of a story. It may add or detract from the original facts of an event, but may also bring a higher level of understanding to someone's motives. Or there may be, in some cases, an interesting juxtaposition between what a person says and what he does. And then, by all means, depending again on the level of celebrity of the person, beat the story to death from every conceivable angle.

All this ranting leads to a classic case of celebrity within an unlikely profession and a case where an unknown quantity exists and how a local television news operation looks at both and the end result.

A battalion chief for a local county fire department, over time, had distinguished himself in fighting fires and savings lives. He had been on-camera several times discussing the cause and effect of various fires. He was well known to local newsmen and the men and women in his profession. Another man from Roy, a few miles up the freeway, with a quiet unassuming job, was unknown outside his own neighborhood.

The well-known fireman was arrested when he to went to meet a 13-year-old girl—presumably for sexual purposes—that he met on the Internet. Instead, he was victim of a sting operation. A law enforcement authority had been posing on the Internet as the young girl. The fireman was arrested, booked and jailed. He made bond and a court date was set. The arrest was a lead story on two of the three television stations so that everyone within the station's wattage could be totally informed, roughly three million people—making any chance of rehabilitation or righting a wrong or effectively explaining his side of the story virtually impossible. The man's heroic history was profiled to draw that difference between what appeared to be a double life. And true to their nature, the stations kept at it until every detail was presented. A week later the fireman was arrested again, for shoplifting. Again, an act in conflict with his public persona and an act that was dutifully reported by the media.

During that same period of time, the other lesser-known man from another community just down the road was arrested when he flew to Detroit to meet a mother and her two very young daughters for sexual purposes. Again, "the mother" was an uncover FBI agent and the man was arrested as he stepped off the plane and jailed without bail. An event unreported by the four major TV stations in the market.

Two men, early fifties, using the internet to make their contacts, accused of similar, despicable crimes and arrested in a police sting operation. One was an acknowledged hero, the other, just a common Joe—on the surface. One has his picture all over television, leading the local newscasts…and the other? Never a mention on television. Nada, zero, zip

The end result: The fireman kissed his wife one morning and left for work only to park his vehicle in a field where he asphyxiated himself. The other man, served a little time, paid a fine and went home, with only a few on his block any the wiser.

And, again, as is its nature, the local television led the newscast with the fireman's suicide, rehashing all the details of the original charges again in case anyone missed them the first time around. The man paid the ultimate price for his previous heroism.

I believe it is worthy to mention here that neither man met, touched, fondled, or harassed any of the young women in question. Granted, their fantasies may have been played out had their intended victims not been undercover police. But both could have gotten cold feet when push came to shove. Of course, this may not have been the first time they had participated in some meeting with young girls. But then again, who knows. Who is to judge?

God only knows the Internet has made grown men do things they never considered. Scores are caught everyday in sting operations. It is a tragedy of gigantic proportion.

Should the media have acted any differently? Probably not! Was it fair? Probably not. Was what the men did, right? Absolutely not! But this is truly one of the terrible truths about local television news. The two events just highlight some of the seeming inequities in news coverage. Assisting in the bringing down of local heroes is a sad occupational hazard. It is also a dimension that builds an audience, increases the revenues, and makes some reporters salivate, all at the same time. It ain't pretty and it's a terrible side of news *and* it is not going away.

If a person is not talented enough to be a novelist,
not smart enough to be a lawyer
and his hands too shaky to perform operations,
he becomes a journalist.
Norman Mailer

There is probably a little bit of truth in that for most of us. And there are probably a lot of journalists who should have at least given other professions a closer look. Of all the years I spent in television news I met one person who loved the business more than anyone. I mean *really loved* the business. The problem was that his love of just being a TV reporter took precedence over good judgment, good taste, tried and true journalistic standards and his relationship with the rest of the newsroom. For the life of me I can't remember why I hired him in the first place; perhaps it was that inner light that sometimes shines when you are talking to a prospective employee. Whatever the reason, the man hit the ground running. He was a whirling dervish in and out of the newsroom. One of his more memorable stories took place in a used tire store. I can't remember the details but I and everyone else can never forget that he wore a spankingly clean and pressed white suit, shirt, tie and shoes in the dirtiest used tired store in town…surrounded by stacks and stacks of filthy used tires and interviewing men wearing clothes that hadn't been washed since their mom used a scrub board.

As I recall, the story had all the elements but all we and the rest of the audience could see and remember was the blinding white suit he wore. After I chastised the producer for not alerting me, I ask our man why he wore the suit. He just said, "For *the contrast.*" Somehow this wasn't covered in journalism school. The closest reference I ever read in school was '*don't compete with the story*.'

As the days rolled into a couple of weeks, our man continued to do his work, though somewhat in an unorthodox manner. To be honest with myself I used him as an example of excitement and enthusiasm for the work at hand, something I thought might rub off on others. This didn't endear me to the newsroom but the audience loved it. The whole matter came apart when our man wrangled himself a ride on a cargo-type plane as part of an Air Force training session open to the public. Again, it was a reasonably routine exercise but the media still covered it. (They'll take anything that happens on a weekend.) With our man as the only reporter *on* the plane, filming the *inside* of a routine function had some merit. But as I was admiring his creative flair, he did the dumbest thing in the history of electronic journalism.

On the day before he rustled up a ride on the plane he had 500 flyers made up to take along. These weren't the post-it size, no sir ree, only the 8½ X 11 size would do, with his name, the television station, a short message and the time of the newscast. To say this boy was enthusiastic about his work and had a natural flare for self-promotion was like watching the late Bill Veeck (…as in wreck), demonstrate his ploys to fill baseball stadiums.

Veeck, as owner of the St. Louise Browns, once sent a little person (Eddie Gaedel) to pinch hit (he got a walk) in a major league ball game. But this was only one of a couple of dozen other stunts he organized to bring in the fans… but in the process pissed off officials and owners of organized baseball. In any case, our reporter must have read Veeck's book. The problem is that while Veeck brought' em in…our man, if allowed, would take' em out.

After the initial function of the Air Force exercise had been completed, our man took his 500 leaflets and threw them out of the plane at 3,000 feet. To the chagrin of our station, even though intended observers picked them up, the city's two newspapers and the other two TV stations in town also found them and we never heard the end of it. Years later, desert rats are still finding them.

The message on the leaflet was derisive to the other media in that they *"… missed the essence of the story and to watch Channel 4 that night for the real story."* Well, that night on the news was the story alright but for the other stations and the newspapers it was less about the Air Force exercise and more about our "stunt" with the fliers. Besides having the other media coughing up fur balls over their glee, I also got a call from the EPA. Before I could even sit our man down for a talk, I had to send him back to the desert to pick up as many of the leaflets as he could find. He searched the desert for several hours but only found a few. The rest became collector items, shelter for the rodents and reading material for prairie dogs and rattlesnakes.

Promoting the news took on a whole new meaning. We diligently tried to keep as low a profile as possible for a couple of months until memories faded or in the retelling of the story people eventually forgot which station it was that did the deed. God bless short memories.

It is never painless to fire anyone. It was always easier when you are so angry at them you want to throw them bodily out the door. But how do you fire a man who loved his work soooooooo much? In the middle of my thought process the dilemma solved itself. Our man, never a great one to know the true principles of the business, walked into my office wearing a very nice and somewhat fancy watch. It was digital but had some flashy embellishments. I didn't make a comment at the time but later when I checked with the assignments editor to ask who was assigned to what, he ran through the story each reporter was covering and almost casually said the our man had run across a business that was on the edge of "new and exciting gizmos," etc. and was doing a story on what was new on the electronic horizon. The watch suddenly reappeared in my rear view vision. I called our man into the office and asked where he got the watch. Without missing a beat he said he was doing a story on a business that was on the edge of "new and exciting gizmos"…and what was "new on the electronic horizon"…and *they gave me a watch as an appreciation for doing the story."*

It is amazing how someone could be so creative and aggressive and a fair writer, yet be so damn stupid when it came to the ethics of his profession. All of us may have made our share of mistakes but, even the most controversial journalists would never consider taking a bribe for doing a story. The story is its own reward. True journalists may fabricate facts, recreate a scenario or worship at the altar of Howdy Doody, but will never take a bribe. The sad thing about our man is that he didn't know there was anything wrong with it. The leaflet drop was small potatoes. Without batting an eye, I told our man that he was fired and the story, with or without him, would not see the light of day… and to return the watch. He profusely apologized but understood and asked me for a recommendation as he moved on. Amazing!!!

6.

**More than journalistic integrity,
more than spectacular production techniques
more than wide ranging coverage
---it is the Anchor who carries a station's news image.**

Hear no evil, speak no evil,
and you'll never be a television anchorman
Dan Rather
Former Anchorman

If you sit at an anchor desk long enough, you'll *hear* it all, *see* it all and *say* it all. The television anchorman/woman is in a unique position to be the traffic cop at the crossroads of the world or, at the very least, of your community. Everything has to pass by, through, in front of or around him/her before anyone else gets a shot at it. Whether the story drips blood…or tears of joy, the anchor is the first to speak, the first to share, the first to get your attention. The subtle *voice* and the *look* will set the tone for the story to follow. It is said that Frank Sinatra gave every *word* in a song special attention, delivering proper inflection and assigning it to its appropriate place to evoke the intended impression. A television anchor should do no less. The better they do it, the more involved and acquainted they are with that particular news of the day…and the more acceptance they'll receive from the viewers. Some anchors do it very well and some are so mechanical that they kill invitation and intent. The one seemingly inconsistent factor is that the anchor can sound great, presenting great professionalism…and still be unacceptable to a viewing audience. They may not like his personality or the way he looks or they may detect an arrogance that is offensive. The camera is a brutal taskmaster.

Anchors may, at times, be the center of the universe but it comes with a price. If the ratings are down, anchors are the first ones to get the blame. They can't have a bad day. They have got to be *up* for every newscast. They must look as good as they sound. The rest of the world can have a bad hair day or lament the break up of a marriage or relationship and even act a little goofy and everyone in the office will be sympathetic and cut some slack, but the anchor better *always* look great, banter easily with his/her co-anchor, seem interested in every story and be on top of his/her game in every way… despite the fact his wife had, that very morning, set fire to his house, shot his dog, wrecked his new 90-thousand dollar Mercedes, wiped out his bank account and ran off with the station's weatherman. And if that isn't bad enough, the ratings may be in the dumper and for an anchor *that is* the true kiss of death. The rest he can handle.

The ratings subject the anchor to *the people* and there is only so much he or she can do to grab and keep their attention, short of mooning the viewers every night. Yet, with all the responsibility of being an anchor, it is still a position to which all other reporters in the newsroom seem to aspire. Someone may be the best work-a-day journalist on the street but part of him/her has an eye on that anchor chair. It's amazing how an ego can convince its owner of almost anything. I've had reporters come to me when there is a rare anchor slot open and all but beg me for a chance to sit on the set and give it a shot. The truth is, practically every reporter can do the mechanics of the job, but once in the chair they realize in short order that it is not as easy as it appears. They can even sound good and look good but every little mannerism, every movement of the head, every tick is magnified a dozen times, and worse, every shred of their personality suddenly goes on display. If there is a hint of arrogance, of having a threatening nature, being stuffy, being nervous, being out of their element— anything that will make a viewer uncomfortable—an anchor's days are numbered. It's a profession that is not for wimps.

Oh, there are compensations. Anchors get paid better than anyone else in the newsroom, including the news director, and nearly all of management, sometimes all of them put together. There is also a celebrity status that comes with the job. It may sound very attractive but the fact is the anchor does more than his share of the heavy lifting. The good ones make it look all easy. And it isn't just the news with which they have to deal. I don't know how many of us could stand up to the public scrutiny; every curl in our hair (if we have any), every speck of makeup, every tooth in our head, every knot in every tie, the color, print and pattern of every shirt-suit-slacks or skirt, every smile, every frown, every word we utter, every stumble...all are on display and all are checked out by every viewer on every newscast. If you wouldn't mind this sort of exposure, there is place for you in the city zoo to display your impenetrable skin to the public.

One of the most impressive performances I saw while on a consulting trip to Albania was an anchorman at TeleArberia in Tirana. I watched his work in the studio while standing behind the camera and noticed he *never* looked down at his copy and he even subtlety used his hands from time to time. Not a lot, just enough to make a point here and there. I was encouraged because I thought the station had invested in a teleprompter, a rare commodity in Albania. Except, where did they place it? It wasn't part of the camera or set above or below it. So, during a newscast, I cautiously walked around on the far side of the studio to see where the anchorman might be looking and still maintain eye contact with the camera. The answer was simple enough. There *was* no teleprompter. The guy *memorizes* every newscast before he goes on air. *He memorizes the whole damn thing!* Every newscast! A sterling performance! The copy was in front of him but he never, ever looked down! Bravo! I've seen guys that can look down at the copy and grab a few lines but never the whole story, much less the whole newscast. And some anchors who are very familiar with a story might ad lib an extra line or two but then quickly revert back to the copy in front of him or the teleprompter. Memorizing the whole newscast twice a day? That's akin to a high wire act without a net at least ten times a week. Unbelievable!

> *Passion is the element in which we live;*
> *without it, we hardly vegetate.*
> Lord Byron

Byron may have been referring to all of us, but in this business, passion seems to have the inside track on a certain species, i.e. the television anchor. Without the passion, the anchor will, indeed, resemble a stick of celery more than a committed professional excited about his work. Somehow, passion *is* the one defining quality of an anchorman. Maybe that's why every young man or woman wants to be one. Passion flourishes in the young, guides and directs in the more mature years and is the sustaining factor for life in the settling years of our lives. Without passion, there is no such thing as television newscasts. The anchors, producers, editors and reporters need it to be accepted and the viewers demand it when they take a slice of their lives to sit in front of a TV set when they could be doing or watching something else. Passion gets us to the next step.

I once had a viewer come into the station and tell me that all his friends and neighbors think he should be an anchorman. Seems he did all the voice work on programs and projects for his church and its 150 members. He truly felt he had some of the needed qualifications. Maybe it was the wrong day to catch me but I had heard too many other versions of the same story. Rather then go into an Anchorman 101 discourse and explain the job description, journalistic qualifications or the dozens of nuisances needed to be an anchorman, I just called the production manager to get the set ready for an audition, then ripped about five minutes worth of copy from the Associated Press wire service, told him to get familiar with the copy…and to meet me in the studio. The camera was fired up and the set lit. I told him just to look into the camera and imagine he was reading copy for the evening news. He did and then I took him back into my office where we looked at the playback. After we watched the tape he looked at me, shrugged and got up and left without saying a word. I didn't stop him.

We wish her all the best...right up to a point.

Brian Williams, NBC evening anchor,
on The Today Show's Katie Couric
moving to CBS to become anchor of the Evening News

One might ask why anyone would give up something that has served them so magnificently for fifteen years and paid them so extreeeeeeeemly well and then move into uncertain, untried territory. There have been other women who have shared a network anchor desk with a fellow co-anchor but never one to be the single anchor. Whether male or female, local or national, being an anchor is quite unlike any other job, in or out of journalism. It is the crème de la crème of occupations. Katie Couric knows that the move was fraught with traps filled with man-eating tigers ready to pounce, and competitors like Williams anxious to introduce her to the new game of network news hard ball. But Couric also saw beyond the obvious. She recognized that being an anchor of a major newscast is more than a job. It is a mission, an appointment, a rendezvous with some personal destiny. It is the top of the mountain. Network news presidents are among her subjects. The all men's club has been broken by Katie and now has since been joined by Diane Sawyer on ABC, a cross, says an older viewer, between Dame May Whitty and Hanna Montana. Whatever, she also brings looks, professionalism and experience to the task. Of course there *are* those who bow to no one, especially those within the journalistic industry, who aren't afraid to take a shot at anyone. Maureen Dowd, who kowtows to no-one—presidents on down—wrote that…"*...so now* (with her 15 million dollar contract) *we'll see if Katie Couric can be trusted with the Herculean task of appearing on camera for five or ten minutes a night, reading a teleprompter.*" As one prominent Republican has said…"No-one wields a knife like Maureen." The fact is that Couric did a fine, credible job as an anchor for the duration of her contract and then moved on to other pastures, to be replaced by another male.

126

Kicking Katie around had been a parlor game for some people for fifteen years and it only got worse as a network news anchor…however, she saved her money line for an interview a month before she took over the CBS anchor chair. In an interview, she said that… *"The biggest job isn't telling people what happened. It's getting them to understand why they should care."* One would only hope that every local reporter puts that line under his/her pillow at night. Maybe they'll come closer to understanding what it is that they do and what it is that they expect from their viewers. Of course there is *always* the valid idea of *informing* their subjects...but in some stories they should help those same people understand why it is so important they should care. It is probably one of the more central functions of a reporter during his/her waking hours. Sadly, when reporters do a story that makes the viewers care about what is being presented, only a few of them realize the service they have performed and then unconsciously slip back into their old habits and routines.

Anchors are alien from nearly every other job in the world. Whether Couric or Joe Smurd in Butte, Montana, they recognize the paradox of their effort is really an example of teamwork shared by dozens to prepare and present the news… yet is perceived by too many viewers as an individual effort. Intuitively, viewers know it is the end result of an *incredible* endeavor on the part of a lot of people. But if the anchor has a nasal quality to his/her voice or has a nervous tick, the viewer will turn away from the whole show, even *if* it is an incredible endeavor on the part of a lot of people. Being an anchor includes not only a lot of work but brings along interesting dimensions to the job: journalism, oratory, cosmetology, dental hygiene and haberdashery all rolled into one. Couric knows it, Smurd knows it.

For beginning journalists, the goal to be an anchor is a beacon in the distance. For the rising reporter, it is that foggy dream that never goes away. For the vastly experienced and older reporter it can be the one ship that will never set sail. .

In England, anchors are called *news readers*, no pretense about what or who they are. In the U.S., network anchors are generally both newsreaders and journalists. (In truth, in some markets an anchor never sees the outside of a studio.) There is a certain period of newscast preparation for any responsible U. S. anchor, local or national. Getting familiar with the scripts, talking to the field reporters involved in a particular newscast, doing some re-writing to fit his/her style, developing handoffs to weather and sports (that's right, it's not always off the top of their heads), and meeting with the news director and others intimately occupied with the news content. Throw in the dreaded consultants who seem to have the answer for everything by dictating every action from content to style to makeup. (An anchorman doesn't suddenly start to wear a warm, fuzzy sweater vest because he personally likes it. The idea is always try to give an anchor more warmth, even if he or she doesn't personally possess it. I once had an anchor that was in love with his black and green checked sports coat. It took an edict from on high to get rid of the damn thing; the point being that anything that is going to draw attention away from the news content is expendable.) And some anchors may have to read more than a couple of newscasts a day. In essence they have a long way to travel in each eight-hour shift and a short time to get there.

The paradox of anchors and the newsroom is harsh reality. The weight of the newsroom hangs heavy on the anchor's shoulders. The assignments editor, news room manager, producer(s), editors and reporters can be the most experienced, the most aggressive and the best writers on the planet and still be second or third in the market if the audience doesn't like the sound of the anchor's voice or hates his black and green checked sports coat. An undernourished newsroom that has never been first at anything but has an anchor that reaches out into a viewer's living room and makes loves to everyone in the room, may garner the number one spot in the market. Fair? Of course not…but that is way the game is played. Look good and sound good! Do that and you're at least half way home.

> *Now there is no way out or into Lebanon*
> *as Israeli air strikes destroy*
> *the last road to Syria!*
>
> Brian Williams
> NBC newscaster
> Opening words to a nightly newscast

> *There is good news tonight!*
>
> Gabriel Heater
> Network Radio Newscaster
> Opening words to every newscast

Two generations apart… a dramatic departure in style to the opening words of a newscast. As mentioned earlier in the book, growing up and spending a lot of time with my grandfather meant I had to listen to the news, especially Mr. Heater. Everything stopped when he came on the radio.

My grandfather and most of the country loved to hear this dean of network radio anchors start the news with his famous byline. If it was a day a tornado wiped out Seattle, he would find a place in the newscast to use it. He was at his most popular when the U.S. was mired in a world war and he wanted to give his listeners something they could hold on to…no matter how gloomy the news was coming from the battle fields. No such luck these days. Mr. Williams and his colleagues hit us right between the eyes with the most dismal thing happening in the world. There is no warming up to disaster and leaving very little to hold on to. Any evening newscast usually puts you in such a funk you wonder what the world is coming to…and it isn't much different watching the opening of any *local* newscast. You'd think that civilization was, indeed, collapsing. In a new century, good news is hard to come by in any newscast, much less finding someone who has the nerve to say "… *there is good news tonight.*" And as long as there is no good news, the viewers at least want it from someone they trust, someone who wears well every night. For over four decades, one local market found such a person.

Sale Lake City is a unique market, in that it is as *personality* oriented as it is *news* oriented. KSL Television's advantage is that it held on to its anchor for over forty years. A genuine, indisputable, unadulterated icon. Dick Nourse was an anchorman at the same station longer than anyone has anchored a major newscast at a single station, on the same channel, anywhere in the world. I repeat…*he was an anchor longer at one station and channel than any anchor anywhere in the world…ever.* And he was originally a walk-on. Now a days, stations search for an anchor the way the Dallas Cowboys search for a quarterback.

Dick's entry into the business may have been happenstance but he richly deserves every accolade to come his way. He has seen it all, including a tour of reporting duty in View Nam where he interviewed Utahns and got their perspectives on the war. In Salt Lake City he reported on the dedication of a spanking new 'Metropolitan Hall of Justice' and 39 years later, reported on its destruction by demolition teams to make room for a new one. And he weathered every management and consultant upheaval; from being upset about the way he combed his hair to the way he read the newscast.

Because of the incredible amounts of cash paid to consultants, management insists that their suggestions be followed to the letter. Dick had heard enough 'suggestions' over the years to make a sane man crazy, yet survived by keeping his focus on why he was there in the first place. He knew that a *suggestion* by the consultants is akin to Tony Soprano hinting to his henchmen that something should be adjusted or that someone should be eliminated. Consultants are a case for another book so will leave it at that. Sadly, consultants are not about being a responsible pipeline of information to the consumer. They are about numbers, pure and simple. And if those consulting distractions weren't enough, Dick was laid up with two bouts of cancer. He was more than a survivor. He is deserving of a bust in an Anchorman's hall of fame. Heaven knows he made the station a ton of money and served as the catalyst for a so-so news department in the beginning to become one of the most honored and revered news departments in the country.

An anchor is an anchor not just because he anchors the newscast everyday…but because he is the anchor of the whole news operation. Everyone ties their tether line to a strong anchor and then bats the ball wherever they want; knowing it always comes back to the anchor. Once you have your anchor set in place, life is a little easier. The anchor is the frame around which everything else functions or smolders.

The irony of the Nourse home base, KSL-TV, is that when Dick was first put on the air, the station got lucky, though it certainly didn't know it at the time. The previous anchor, one John Willis, had been brought in from L.A. He said he was tired of the 'rat race' and was looking for a slower pace in a market where his family could thrive, etc. etc. etc. KSL-TV offered him the moon, a star or two and a position in broadcast heaven. Nice guy, smart, good looking, nice voice, hometown look, settled, married…seemed a good fit. But the fit quickly became a squeeze play by Willis. Seems the L.A. boy was between jobs and KSL needed an anchor. Willis took it but longed for the smog and celebrity only L.A. could afford. In the meantime, Dick—who had originally been hired as a board announcer for off-camera work and then read public service announcements on Romper Room—was summoned to read the weekend newscasts. Willis read the news during the week but on weekends he fled for L.A. to reconnect with broadcast cronies. The station thought he was just going back to visit his family and help them prepare for the move to Salt Lake City. It didn't take Willis long to realize that he had to be in sunny California during a weekday to be effective in finding a job in L.A. So he told the management at

KSL he needed more time to help the family prepare for the move, which included selling his home. Dick was then asked to read the news on Friday as well as the weekend. But even Friday wasn't enough time to strike employment gold so Willis stayed Monday as well. Now Dick was reading the news four days a week. And then the inevitable happened. John Willis was hired by some L.A. facility and he lost no time in breaking his contract to KSL. It took him about ten minutes to pack up and leave, in his words, *this "two bit market."* The station was back to square one, with no permanent anchor. The idea was to leave Dick on until they found someone else. Thankfully, they drug their feet long enough to see that Dick might just have the legs to run the whole race. There was a realization that Dick was a good anchorman and getting better all the time. The search for a new anchor ground to a halt and the station decided to put all its marbles in Dick's basket.

Over the years KSL always had the reputation of "buying" its talent from the competition. Before management saw the virtue in that practice, they tried to use creative promotion or sometimes, create a super sized individual and catapult him into stardom, leaving any vestige of natural talent at the gate. Take the case of Lynn (Rocky) Rockwood, smart, knowledgeable, affable, the state's top tennis player, but not what you would call an experienced sports anchor. As one observer said...*he has the brains, but not the tennis balls for television.* But KSL, true to form, said it was going to weave silk out of ordinary cloth.

In the meantime, across the street was a news, weather, sports anchor team that couldn't be touched, silk purses all the way. KSL's research found that the station's strength lay in its weather and sports anchors, Bob Welti and Paul James. The initial thinking was to buy 'em all, including the news anchor, and bring them back across the street. Surely the relatively new anchorman, Dick Nourse, would understand...and of course, "Rocky" Rockwood, one month on the job, would certainly stand aside. There was one problem...the news anchor across the street said no. He didn't like KSL, wasn't a Mormon—not that that was a prerequisite to be happy there, but it might help—and elected not to jump ship. Nourse was safe but the weather and sports anchors would go on the block. The station absorbed the weatherman in the announcing ranks...but Rocky, freshly chained to a three-year contract and plenty of promotion and promise, soon received the inevitable visitor from management. It probably went something like this...

"Of course, Rocky, I'm sure you see our point of view. Here we have a chance to get the number one sports personality in the market…but we are going to make it right with you. We will give you three months severance and our enduring friendship and respect." To which Rocky said something like…*"Save your words and your three month severance. My attorney will be in touch."*

Mr. Rockwood ultimately was paid the entire three-year contract and a substantial punitive amount, enough to allow for a comfortable living while he pursed his doctorate at the University of Utah. Dr. Rockwood eventually became director of the Salt Lake County recreation programs. Nourse, Welti, & James took over the number one position in the market in the first rating book after the change, with Channel Four falling to third place.

Forty odd years later, both stations maintained the same position in the rating with Nourse outlasting everyone on both sides of the street; the walk-on with no experience who just happened to be in the right place at the right time, but had the mettle, the skill and the guts to survive as no anchor on earth has survived in the business. He watched the comings and goings of news, weather and sports anchors for nearly half a century, including a father-son weather combo, a first anywhere in the country. Some viewers had taken to calling them Augie Doggie and Doggie Daddy. Whatever you called them…they did know their weather. They lived it, ate it, breathed it…and Doggie Daddy even dressed for it. You knew when it was going to snow because he wore a white sport coat. Today his son repeats the practice.

The one continuing element all stations seem to have in common is trying to find the right chemistry between anchors and their audience. For this they use focus groups—made up of 7 to 10 complete strangers—to make the final decisions. The stations look for any advantage to make the right choice(s). When management doesn't trust their own judgment, they bring in a butcher, baker, teacher, bus driver or fork lift operator to sit around a table and then show them a bunch of videos of existing local anchors, potential anchors or current anchors in other parts of the country looking for a change. These ordinary folks—using good old native instincts, gut reactions and whatever else that turns them on—then watch and reveal who they like and for what reasons. Louis B. Mayor of Hollywood fame said he would decide on what actor to put in a film by the *"feeling he felt in his ass."* One hopes the decisions made in a focus group would come from a little higher level.

132

Over the years the gymnastics performed by news departments in Utah have been just short of pure desperation. The best other stations can hope for when competing against Dick, was second place. They spent so much time juggling anchor slots they resembled Wiley E. Coyote chasing Mr. Nourse down the road, with the same success. Anchors will jump from one station to another and new men and women will be brought in from out of state to give the cast a fresh look only to realize that the audience doesn't want someone new. It wants someone who will be there forever and never leave their side. Anchors are like a favorite uncle or aunt who sits down in the living room and tells them what's been going on in the world. And then they leave without   making a mess or bumping into the furniture, announcing they'll be back the next day. One interesting note: When Nourse retired, the station dropped to Number 2.

An anchor is the closest thing that electronic journalism, local or national, has to a rock star, so there is a natural curiosity about how they conduct their lives, particularly when they screw up. Salt Lake City's Channel Four once had a weekend anchor who spent his off time romancing several married ladies. This had gone on for some time and, as always happens in such cases, there is such a thing as too much of a good time. One Friday afternoon, the anchor in question received a phone call from a very irate and threatening husband. He was told that if he was caught anywhere near the caller's wife, he would be shot on sight…and then hung up. To say the sins of the anchor had caught up with him would be understating the case. His main problem was that he didn't know *which* husband had called, so he curtailed all activities for the next few days.

That weekend, still nervous as a man trying to escape a rabid dog, the anchor went about his on-camera duties of reading Saturday and then Sunday's news. The studio staff took notice of his unsteady delivery but the show had to go on. In the control booth, the technical director (TD)—in charge of camera movements, inclusion of proper news film/tape and commercial placement— also believed the anchor's mind was somewhere other than in a TV studio. On Sunday night, the anchor—still nervous as a cat in a room full of rocking chairs —was anxiously trying to get through a live read when one of the studio's incandescent lights blew out, something resembling a gunshot.

As the technical director was watching his monitor in the control room, he said the anchor *just disappeared*. Slightly panicked, the TD cut to the customary wide shot of the entire studio before going to a commercial break and there, for the entire world to see, was the anchor, on all fours, crawling away from the podium that held his news copy. During the commercial break, the TD and the cameramen had to talk, beg, cajole and threaten to get him back to the podium. He practically had to be carried back and then stood up like a mannequin in a department store window. When the commercials were over, he stood there looking like someone had just hit him between the eyes with a crow bar. Miraculously, he managed to string enough words together to finish the newscast. He left the market two weeks later, minus any of his married lady friends.

Salt Lake City, in particular, has a habit of chewing up anchors. It is a very family oriented market with a predominant Mormon population. It is a culture with a history of knowing how to survive. They recognize and appreciate congressmen who can make tough decisions, governors who aren't afraid to challenge the electorate and other elected officials who are not shrinking violets and unafraid to get their hands dirty. And they like longevity in their officials *and* in their anchors.

Viewers know the stations generally cover the same big national stories and highlights of local news…but as earlier stated, Salt Lake City is a more *personality*-oriented market. The folks want the news but want it from the person with whom they feel the most comfortable, really not unlike most cities in the country.

Of course, all station managers and news directors in every city say that journalistic integrity and coverage capability are more important than the personalities. That's great humility on paper; a station can have the best coverage in town, but if the folks at home don't like who is presenting it, they'll turn the channel in a heartbeat. Pitifully, it is a truth that sticks in management's throat like a chicken bone. Throughout the newsroom there is an undeclared feeling that there is entirely too much emphasis and attention on the anchors, and the credit he or she receives. They feel the anchors, most of the time, sit on the tail end of the hard work by the photographer who had been up for twenty four straight hours and a reporter who lives and dies with his/her story. And the anchor gets paid more for reading the introduction to the story than the combined salaries of both the reporter and photographer.

The inequities shout throughout a newsroom but the reporters, photogs, editors, etc. have long ago accepted their fate.   Besides, they have their own problems, one of which is the *Seventh Terrible Truth*...

7.

Television is a triumph of equipment over people.

This Truth was first uttered by Fred Allen in 1953 but is still applicable today, primarily because the technology is changing so rapidly. Seemingly, every other day a new piece of equipment becomes available to television news departments and each seems to have a bearing on how the news will be presented. Even our phones have video camera capability. Ironically, today's newscasts using all the new tools don't proportionately provide any more information than was given ten or twenty years ago. The difference is in the presentation; today's newscasts are slicker than scum on a Louisiana swamp. There are fewer mistakes, it's more pleasant to the eye, and information is arranged in a more acceptable manner. There are spectacular graphics which reinforce the information being presented and, of course, there are the live shots from just about everywhere. Still, television trips, stumbles, and often falls on its face, but is trying harder than a unemployed actor to get your attention and insure that watching a newscast will somehow enhance your life and provide needed information on a day to day basis, however limited or expansive it might be. More than ever, judgment plays a larger role than ever.

> *There is more to life than increasing its speed.*
> Mahatma Ghandi

The one big edge TV has over print...*is* speed. Reporters may not be able to delve into every single facet of a piece of news but TV news can more rapidly present the information in a way that will make it more interesting to watch and easier to understand. For decades the talk has been about speed, getting today's information out yesterday. After years of slowly clawing its way up the information industry's slippery slopes, the genie is finally out of the bottle. Technology is pushing us in directions we only fantasized about last week. As mentioned, our cell phones are now TV sets and newsrooms are latching onto all new technology like it's the Holy Grail. Everyone wants to be the firstist with the mostist. It's all about speed and graphics. Ghandi be damned and Dick Tracy was a hack with his flimsy two way wrist watch. After all, why read the paper when the boys and girls in TV can make up for their lack of information—at which newspapers excel—by putting all the bells and whistles in a story to titillate and fascinate the mind? There may not be a lot of new information but the video sure looks good.

Every electronic journalist knows the newspapers offer more information and do it better on a daily basis. Technically speaking, newspapers offer stories, renderings and headlines in basically the same way for the last two hundred years, with photography making a steady appearance in the late 1800s. Not so the people in television. Every new piece of equipment changes the approach, the presentation, the selection of information and the corresponding viewer reaction to it.

The more technology becomes available the more irresistible it is to use every nano-byte of it. This may be good in selling coffee, clothes or cars…but working too hard to sell a story is another matter. More and more the visual is so powerful, so enticing, so unique that it dictates where the story is placed, and the allotted time given to it, even if it has nothing to do with our lives or our futures.

Believe me, if there is a new way to do or convey something, it will find its way into a newscast. But still, for all the magic of technology, if a viewer has a tennis match or can't pull him/herself away from a stubborn weed patch in a garden, he/she won't miss a beat if the newscast is missed. Certainly, the challenge before all broadcasters is to be a continuing and positive force in the unfolding lifestyle of all Americans. And always, journalists have to remind themselves of a few essentials to make sure they are adequately representing not only themselves but the viewers as well.

The 'live' shot is the latest ploy and probably best innovation in a newscast to keep a viewer interested. It's expensive to do and it rarely provides more information than before but it gives the newscast a snappier look and the illusion that it presents information that you wouldn't get otherwise. (The key word here is *illusion*.) The technology that makes it possible wasn't created overnight and is a perfect example of the evolutionary unfolding of TV News. It took a while to work out the chinks but now stations are more proficient and give the impression that the 'live' shot isn't being done for the sake of a live shot. Frankly, it is…but that's another truth. Of course the "live" shot really earns its accolades when it captures important news as it unfolds before your very eyes…and today's equipment makes it all possible. But it's defining the word *important* that gets producers into trouble.

Any news director will tell you that "live" shots are being picked for their news value and not for their vices. The problem is—he really believes it. The truth is that live shots are done mostly for the cosmetics of a cast, not for the added information it is suppose to give. Every newscast has 2 to 3 'live' shots. Maybe *one* might lend some new information or immediacy or insight to the story. The *others* are done to add eyeshade, lip-gloss and some costume jewelry to the story.

Still, surveys by competent companies say that the viewers feel there is greater credibility to the story when there is someone outside providing a "live" report, preferably standing in a rainstorm. Never mind that the story probably happened sometime during the daylight hours but the reporter hangs out for several hours waiting to do the live report at ten p.m. It's done not because there is new information about the story but because it looks cool to have a live reporter at night against a backdrop of what happened, even if, most of the time, the police or whoever have mopped up had gone home. And it doesn't have to be an accident or a crime scene. It could be in front of a building where something happened or some decision was made earlier in the day. The technology makes it possible to move in different directions at the same time and give a proximity that is always preferable in any newscast.

There was a time when equipment, or the lack of it, planted our feet in concrete, making it impossible to be doing anything that remotely resembled creativity, immediacy, urgency or priority. Once the idea of a remote broadcast was possible for everyone, *wherever* they were, our world changed, the industry changed, the viewers changed…but the *information* remained basically the same, from murders to the mundane, from fires to fights, from invention to shifting ideas. It was just that all this information was presented differently. And there are some of us who wonder if all the changes and all the new technology are really making journalists more effective in presenting news to the public. Oh, you can safely bet some of the nightly footage is more dramatic and the era of live television is certainly here to stay. "Live" shots abound and there is the impression that the viewers are actually better informed about information that is critical to them about their community. There is nothing like using a helicopter to tape a mountain rescue or a chase down the freeway or a home fire, most of which are broadcast live. All of it is so commonplace that it is an anticipated lead in the nightly news, every night. One might think that both the journalist and the viewer should pay homage to the forerunners of this whole business of local news. If they do, they have a funny way of showing it.

Today's razzmatazz dazzles us so much that we've actually been duped about what is really happening in our community. After all, this spectacular stuff—car crashes, petty crime, subjects for flashy video—has been happening all along but we just haven't seen it up front and personal…so maybe it's time for reflection. Are we now better informed? Can we now better discuss unfolding issues that truly affect our lives? Has technology replaced a hardy question and answer session between a competent reporter and someone who is either deceiving or helping the community in critical areas? Has the thrill of technology erased time that could be better used for truly important news? Has technology interrupted the reporter's dance with the viewer once too often?

One might accuse me for being a little nostalgic in comparing the past with the present, but I'm not. I see how technology with graphics can explain stories as never before, how information, properly presented, can raise local news to a level that will touch our lives. We have held out hope for real change, for real professionalism, for real empathy with community issues, for courage…but our patience is running thin. Today, everything *is* being presented better, slicker, faster and even more understandable. (It's what *is not* being covered that is lacking.)

Credit also belongs to management who stepped up and encouraged the purchase of the latest technology. They understood its importance and how it could ultimately affect the bottom line. Of course…the bottom-line! Yes, there was, there is…a savage devotion to that bottom line. It's a business, to be sure, and some owners and managers are meeting their responsibilities to a waiting public. But, in the past, there were some classic holdouts.

As mentioned, I started in the television industry in a small station in Missoula, Montana. KMSO was owned by Art J. Mosby, a hard man with a buck. Asking him for a dime an hour raise could be tantamount to lifetime banishment from the station. His background alone would make a book. When he died, commentator Paul Harvey did a considerable bio on the man. Harvey once worked for Mosby and credits him with a boost to his career. Unfortunately, of those who worked for him, Harvey was only one of a few who rose above the ordinary.

Mosby was notorious for his penurious ways. Once, when he wanted to go to Chicago to an NAB conference he asked his chief engineer to go with him, except that he wanted the poor guy to drive the company Volkswagen to Chicago from Missoula, Montana because once there they could use it instead of the "expensive" cabs. And while he was staying in the Ritz, the engineer could find a room at the YMCA. A put-on? Mosby never kidded. Never! Not when it came to money. He made the proposal with a straight face and never batted an eye. After a couple days of thought, the engineer begged off, saying the miniscule sized staff was already short handed and needed him. Mosby shrugged and went alone.

Mosby got his start operating a small hardware store in Missoula. What he didn't have in stock as requested by a customer he would run out the back door of his own store to the store across the street, buy the item, then run back and sell it to the customer with a 15% mark up. As radio became more and more popular he employed the same routine until he made enough to build up stock of his own. Eventually he started KGVO Radio in Missoula and later, KMSO-TV. The history of both is unimportant, except in terms of money spent to keep each on the air.

The problem with KMSO-TV was that it was off the air half the time. Even though the studio was in a downtown location, the broadcast antenna, on top of Missoula Mountain, was constructed of a pole, baling wire, Aunt Ada's corset and some chewing gum. It was manned and maintained by two 'engineers' who alternated living and working in a small shack next to the antenna. Finally, after enough pressure from the staff and half of Missoula, Mosby finally relented and had RCA put up a new antenna that was over 150 feet high. After several days of work, the job was deemed complete...and the engineers headed back down the mountain.

We in the downtown studio were elated at the picture quality and felt assured of a long run without troubles. But, about 20 minutes after signing on with our new antenna, the picture suddenly went to black and then nothing but snow.

With our two-way communication system to the mountaintop, we tried for several minutes to reach our man babysitting the new system. We eventually learned that as the RCA boys were winding their way to the bottom of the mountain, our man on top of the mountain, feeling confident with the new arrangement left the engineer's shack for the outhouse 30 yards away. (There *was* electricity up there but no plumbing.) While sitting comfortably, enjoying the moment and a magazine, he heard a nerve rattling crash and felt the outhouse move about a foot. With trepidation, he pulled up his pants and slowly opened the door.

There in front of him was the engineer's shack with the new antenna lying squarely across the roof. He would have been under the rubble if he had delayed his mission to see a man about a horse. A postscript to the story: the RCA boys went back up the mountain, re-installed it and again, it fell over. The curse and legacy of Art Mosby was alive, well and getting stronger every day.

> *If we had the right technology back then,*
> *you would have seen*
> *Eva Braun on Oprah and Adolph Hitler on Meet the Press.*
>
> Ed Turner

…and we could have shown them in their own living quarters. Who knows, maybe we could have avoided WWII. Or at least we'd have a better look at a few of the players. Today's newscasts and news programs are smooth as silk. But reaching this flawless era meant years of by-guess and by-golly when building a newscast without the benefit of today's technology was an exercise in futility night after night. There were times when you swore that Larry, Moe and Curly had inhabited the building.

Today, there are a few screw-ups but generally speaking, everything is very professional. Still, whenever you get together a bunch of guys who once put together a newscast on the fly, you'll hear stories that will be told and retold for the ages. The same is true for radio.

My favorite is about a local radio station with a fierce independent spirit. The on-air personalities were sharp with a serrated edge. A morning man they hired from Billings, Montana was the new man in town and quickly forged a place for himself among the station's other heavyweights. He had the morning drive time, which meant that he had to juggle information that included a lot of bantering between himself and others, such as sports, weather, news and traffic. Traffic included a plane in the sky that would feed road and freeway weather conditions and construction blockage. The pilot was also the man with the microphone inside the plane.

The station (KALL) billed itself as the first station in the market to have a live traffic report, beating it's nearest rival, KSL by one day. Traffic reports, at that time, were a novelty in the area but not the rest of the country. As usual, Salt Lake City felt it was time to catch up. KSL Radio heavily promoted its coming inclusion of traffic reports in it's mix of morning and early evening programming. KALL Radio quietly decided to do the same and while it was at it to steal KSL's thunder in the process. The idea was to be the first in the market to offer such a service. So on a quiet Sunday *afternoon* while half the valley was in Church and the other half watching a football game, KALL took to the air, 15 hours *before* KSL was to initiate its own first-of-a-kind-in-the-market traffic report. Cheesy as it may have been, KALL now had forever bragging rights as to who was the first.

Traffic reports aren't without their problems. There are three unpredictable qualities that can alter any well planned intention: the plane, the radio in the plane and the weather. Any one of them, or all falling apart together, can change the program schedule in the studio. On one particular morning, the winter weather was more than challenging. The road to the hanger was snowbound; it took an inordinate amount of time to warm up the plane; the broadcast radio in the cockpit had to be thawed out; all had to be dealt with. Don't ask me to be too technical here. I know just enough to lay out the bare essentials of the story. Ronnie (not his real name) was the pilot/broadcaster. The morning man, Jack Bogut (his real name), was anxious for the first of Ronnie's reports. The weather had compounded traffic and if there was a time for a traffic report, this was it. Ronnie finally got the plane in the air, a half hour late, but his broadcast radio was still thawing out, but he could communicate with Jack on an audition channel (off air) giving him information as to when he might be ready.

During music and commercials Jack pressed Ronnie for a traffic report. Finally, as a commercial ended, he told his listeners that he was going to check with Ronnie for a report and, on an audition channel to Billy, asked if he was ready with a description of weather and traffic. The listeners could hear Jack but not Ronnie. Ronnie, on the audition channel said, *"Yeah…let's go…"*…at which point Jack threw the switch into the program mode (on air), and Ronnie—still thinking he was in an audition (off air) mode—said *"…if I can get this God damn Jap radio to work."*

Well! Jack, known for his quick wit, was momentarily stunned but hastily took up the verbal challenge. He told Ronnie to give a traffic report and later they'd discuss the new friendship agreement between Japan and the United States. For the rest of the morning Jack kept telling his listeners to be alert to the coming repeat of the 45-year-old Pearl Harbor attack on Ronnie's front lawn. A lesser radio personality, without Jack Bogut's quick wit and sense of humor, could have created an enormous problem for the station. Even Ronnie survived his job mainly because Japanese-American locals appreciated the mistake and the handling of it…though Ronnie was never given a personal invitation to any Japanese celebrations at the city's Buddha Temple.

The biggest major change in local news was when videotape replaced film. But it was hardly that easy. The birth of tape was like birth of a child. There is a learning process that is expensive and frustrating…but when it worked, it was wonderful. The advantages are obvious, in terms of cost, speed and convenience.

On the heels of the switch to videotape came the next most dramatic change. In the beginning, as earlier mentioned, when someone being interviewed needed to be identified, the studio crew would make up titling cards with specific names of individuals at the bottom, such as John R. Fox, Director, City Zoo...and then place them on an easel. And then an $85,000 studio camera would be isolated on that easel for the technical director to superimpose Mr. Fox's name on the lower 1/3 of the picture. It was a time consuming pain and often the titling was incomplete by airtime. Little by little, computers and the magicians to operate them changed the whole texture of the newscast. Graphics would soon rule the roost in the most positive way.

News departments now employ full time graphic artists to enhance and reinforce the information in a newscast. Of all the advances in technology the use of spectacular graphics is probably the most valuable. It enables an anchor or reporter to frame his/her information is a way that will make it easier to read and more understandable to the viewer.

Anything that will help an audience comprehend and remember what is being presented is worth every cent it costs to achieve it. It is where technology truly shines. More reassuring is that stations have learned to understand and use their equipment in a more responsible manner. But like anything else, there could be too much of a good thing. Fancy, well-meaning graphics, while pleasing to the eye, can oversell a story of bone jarring *in*significance. Strong willed producers have to constantly be alert to the time and effort taken for each story. Still, this is a *terrible truth* that is becoming less terrible.

While the viewers seem to quietly accept the changes as a matter of course, there are still questions in the minds of some who are concerned about whether the viewers are better off.

> *This boy's makin' more noise than a couple of skeletons throwing a fit on a tin roof.*
> Foghorn Leghorn

In some strange way, noise coming out of the scientists and technicians workshops are reaching a level where viewers are not sure what to expect next. We already have live reports from just about everywhere, graphics that are not only artistic and alluring but a tremendous aid to convey information, an incorporation of pictures from satellites and the technology to zoom in on a single individual in his back yard…and God's only knows what is next from the noisy workshop.

While all visual high jinks embraces and romances an audience—made possible by the wizardry of technology—the jury is still out whether it's an effective way to help the folks in TV land to better understand a story or improve their lifestyle through information learned…*or* is it just fluff to make it more appealing to the eye and anesthetizing to the brain. The flow of a newscast makes it virtually impossible to put too much thought into any one of the stories, so the idea is to make a story look appealing, sound appealing and feel appealing.

The irony is that the world seems to be suffering from an information overload…and it looks likes the technicians have done about all they can do from their end—to bring it to the viewer. With its tongue firmly planted in its cheek, The Onion—a weekly favorite on college campuses—offers a disturbing look at this massive flow of information.

> We now see cases of information-overload across the country—a truly terrifying disease, especially among those who watch excessive amounts of television or read two or more newspapers a day. The result: cynicism, apathy, fatigue, and consistently strained retinas.
>
> Sadly, the country's most informed are the most at risk. These brave but misguided souls continue to live a waking nightmare, still consuming dangerous amounts of information and analysis about their ever-more-complex world.
>
> According to new data, if Americans continue needlessly paying attention to current events at this rate, our nation will completely run out of attention-paying capacity by the summer of 2012.
>
> It's time for America to wake up. Issues like the Iraq war, the Middle East peace process, the debate over intelligent design, influence-peddling in Washington, the fate of Social Security, Hurricane Katrina, and global warming, to name just a few, cannot be paid attention to indefinitely.

Satire may be the best way to look at our world—and survive. We've all learned that there is such a thing as *too much*. There's too much traffic, too much fast food, too much pressure…and especially too much information, so much in fact that too many people have stopped watching local TV newscasts altogether.

Right or wrong, people believe there is too much violence in the news and just don't want to deal with it. It is an argument hard to refute and now, with today's level of technological advances, the viewer can be brought to *where* the violence happened within minutes of *when* it happened, with eyewitnesses only too anxious to tell *what* happened, and some authority explaining *why* it happened…and TV news departments are only too willing to record it all and show you every grisly detail. And half the potential viewers want nothing to do with it.

And then there is the Internet. Some say, it will rescue all the information on a newscast and make it available for even more people, thereby increasing the audience numbers, complete with commercial drop ins, etc. Don't bet the farm on it. If people don't have the interest to watch the news as it is being presented, it's doubtful they'll take the time, on their own initiative, to use the Internet to see what they missed. Critics are betting they will likely only check out the spots that hold a personal interest for them and ignore the rest.

For those who do watch the news, it's a roll of the dice as to whether they'll want more information about what was on television. However, I do believe the Internet will ultimately become a player in the distribution of news, but don't expect some great breakthrough in getting people suddenly interested enough in their world and community to burst through the doors of information providers. An occasional gentle knock on the door would be more likely.

> *We can't quite decide if the world is growing worse*
> *or if the reporters are just working harder*
> Houghton Times

While written with some levity in mind, it still seems to be a statement of reckoning. People wanting to become journalists are generally dependent on their curiosity and the lure of travel, romance, and fame more than it is a response to what is happening in the world at any given moment. Considering what is going on over the last few decades, we could probably use a few more journalists who are dedicated and courageous and have an innate deep-rooted desire to inform the public. Any fool can report an accident or a shooting but it takes a committed journalist to probe the reasons *why* and *discern* some behavioral practices that will determine some future outlook, good or bad. We like to think that kind of dedication would become a wave of the future but realistically, it is highly unlikely. Journalism is a craft that churns out more recruits than are those leaving the profession. The problem is… do we need more reporters out there to remind us how dismal life is on the six continents as well as our own back yards? And it isn't only the number of journalists reminding us of our follies; it is also the number of news outlets serving mankind 24 hours a day that are constantly looking for fresh blood.

One wonders what the future holds for the presentation of news for people both around the world and around the corner. It's hard to believe it can get any crazier than it is today. But you can bet that reporters are ready to jump on any new piece of equipment that comes out of the technicians' workshops. If the past is any indication, the crackerjacks of technology will continue their relentless pursuit to craft new hardware to more creatively broadcast the news. Truthfully, the mechanics of a newscast will continue to change as long as there is such an industry…or until the rest of us are recording what Ms. Brooks calls *the total collapse of journalism.*

8.
Flashing red lights illuminate the stage of a local TV news operation!

Well, a man comes on the 6 o'clock news
Said somebody's been shot, somebody's been abused
Somebody blew up a building
Somebody stole a car
Somebody got away
Somebody didn't get too far, yeah
They didn't get too far.

Toby Keith
The song…'Beer For My **Horses'**

And therein lies what most folks think about the news. As suggested earlier, most surveys show that those who don't watch the news do so because of all the negative stories presented every night. A further survey by the *Project for Excellence in Journalism* reveals that 40% of the newscasts in local TV markets are crime related. Throw in accidents and the figure rises to 50%. So, being too negative is a charge hard to combat. Much of the local TV news *is* negative, but some, occasionally, is genuine and valid, some is also bland explanation, some is exploring, some is enlightening, some is even funny. Not as funny as giving beer to your horses but still, lighthearted and carefree. But let's face it; the local lead stories generally have a red flashing light somewhere in the background.

News is so often a report of conflict,
an account of problems, a thing of the day and even of the minute,
that sometimes I think we make the background darker
and the shadows deeper then they actually are.

Arthur H. Sulzberger

Credit the venerable Mr. Sulzberger who, at least, recognized the media sometimes overdoes a story, putting a more negative slant or spin on it than it needs or is fair. But that's one of the pure pleasures the media have enjoyed since Gutenberg fired up the first printing press or what any editor—TV or newspaper—seems to do with lead stories in particular.

There is a broader concern here than just *what* stories lead the newscasts and exactly *why* they have to take precedence over all other news that truly influences our lives. Is it really our fascination with the crime stories and accidents or is it the avarice in the souls of those who chronicle these events? The bigger question is why do they have to *lead* the newscast day in and day out, every day? I know this is an obvious question but considering what viewers are facing in the world on a day-to-day basis and the questions to which they need answers and the warnings they need to hear, one wonders just what role those lead stories (in the local newscast) play in today's society. Having asked the question, anyone with half a brain knows the answer; it's about money and numbers. The fact that the viewers *might* want more meat on their bun is rarely taken into account. If the newsroom would get away from the statistics fed to them by government officials (local and national) of how well everything is doing and really look at the more specific dimensions of the community and the struggles viewers have in just trying to survive, all the flashing red lights might suddenly lose their glow.

> *When there are two conflicting versions of a story,*
> *the wise course is to believe the one in which*
> *people appear at their worst.*
> H. Allen Smith

People are generally taught from childhood to *believe* in the *best* of people. Journalists, by tradition, by practice and by nature are taught to *look* for the *worst* in people. It is, unfortunately, a sad fact of life…and there are those critics that believe that if this were not the case, our world would be a much better place in which to live. We're taught that people rise to their level of expectation by others. With the podium that journalists use on a daily basis, with people like H. Allen Smith as a mentor, it doesn't seem like our world has much of a chance of turning the corner.

News directors, promotion directors, station managers and consultants have convinced themselves that crime, accidents and the worst in mankind are what the viewer wants and so they happily comply. Crime and punishment, accidents and tragedy are tailor made for TV. The stories are not complex and are easy to cover. In actual fact, they fall in the newsroom's lap. Another no brainer. The evidence that the stories rarely affect the viewer's lives, except for a visceral reaction, does not seem to apply to the station's sense of civic responsibility that is always flaunted before the viewing public with those sanitized promotional spots. After all, it's a lot easier than busting your hump in going out and looking for news that actually makes a difference or is something of which the public may not be aware. It is not a coincidence that some markets are cutting back on their reporting staffs. Finding pertinent news takes time and effort. Better to follow the same old paths. They're wider, well traveled, free of dangerous animals and hidden traps.

On paper, the news media plays the principle role of informing the people of *what* is happening in their community, *what* persons and companies are doing to either solve or create public problems and *what* is being accomplished on their behalf. Also on paper, they are informed about *what* laws are being enacted to protect and help them, *what* facilities are being created to make their lives better, *what* steps are being taken to counter the harmful dimensions in everyday life, *what* information is being presented to help people make critical decisions in their lives, *what* safeguards are being erected for our children, *what* questions are being asked of our city, county, state and national officials to help people in their daily lives, and *what* answers they are providing to those questions, etc. At least in theory that is *what* the media is supposed to do and that is *what* they say they *are* doing. Yes, and I have a pet cricket that chirps Lady of Spain.

We listen and watch each TV station promoting its news department and *never* is there any mention about the accidents and shootings they cover that are put right up front for all to see at the very beginning of nearly every newscast. Typically, the promotions are all about the dazzling information they bring to their viewers—during that short period of time that is left after all the crash-boom-bang stuff—to help them to be better informed citizens. Actually, there are some of the accidents that need to be covered and some of the crime related stories need to be exposed. No one is protesting this type of coverage. It is just the quantity of it, not the quality.

Squander yourself for a worthy purpose!
Edmund Burke

One can only follow Burke's advice if they give a total commitment to a project or idea, with very little thought about personal reward. It is particularly fitting as we try to get a stronger foothold on the 21st Century. Life ain't easy because we live in a world in turmoil and crisis. At the same time there are people and institutions responding to the needs of all mankind as well as addressing smaller pockets of people trying to overcome any number of personal and collective challenges. However, if you watch a local TV newscast you get very little of any of it. The name of the game is to grab the viewer by the throat—so keep the flashing red lights in good working order. A pity! A medium with so much power to inform, enlighten and illuminate instead squanders itself on irrelevance. A pity, indeed.

Keep in mind that after decades of broadcasting the news, the booming question is *why isn't TV local news getting more proficient at presenting information that will bring clarity to community issues? Management* will say because it is already giving the viewer what it wants. The *ownership* will say this is a business and we'll take those steps that will bring us the most viewers, allowing us to raise our advertising rates so that we can make more money keeping the stockholders and investors happy. The *consultants* will say that they have researched the market and have determined what the people will watch. (In truth, it is a cookie cutter plan that is promoted from market to market.) The *newsroom* will say the consultants tell us what to do. Of course, all of this is obvious stuff and probably an exercise in futility by the one asking the question. The astute viewer will recognize that local TV news *is* business as usual. The *very* astute viewer knows that TV news is not taking a step back...nor is it stepping forward. It has gone off on some side road that focuses *not* on explanation, clarification and revelation, but numbers—*viewers and dollars.*

Before the news departments start crying foul, it must be stated that they are very capable of informing and influencing the viewer. It's just the infrequency that disparages what could make them quality news operations. What the viewer needs is more consistency. While the promotion departments are always touting the high standards of the stations, it is high time the news that is broadcast nightly rises to the occasion of its own promotion. The best stuff is always saved for the rating periods and the promotion departments go nuts in running promotional spots at least a week before the stories are aired. The idea is to make it look like this is what the news department does all the time. It doesn't. Not even close. In the rear view mirror all management sees is *more viewers mean more money.* And of course the stations do run investigative reports occasionally outside the rating periods but not with the same flare, frequency, production techniques or sense of importance.

Outside the local newscasts there are the weekly network news magazines that do their usual superb job of examining an issue, though most of the issues examined make only a small impact on our lives. Too often they take up a whole hour dissecting the activity it took to bring a criminal to justice or taking a look into something that, while interesting, doesn't always mean much to the life of the average viewer. Probably the most informed efforts on TV are the morning programs on the network that get into several issues, many of which directly affect the viewers. And throw in Oprah and Dr. Phil and a few others and you have some very constructive programs to gain information about yourself or how to handle a given situation. But again, they are scheduled during times when the audience is spotty and low in numbers. Most people in the country are working and don't have the time until later in the evening.

One has to wonder just what *the fascination is for minor crime stories and less than spectacular accidents* by both news operations and the people who like to watch their efforts on the nightly news. Considering most news operations go for the obvious stories—crime, accidents, etc and high profile stories that are also obvious in their content, the question arises, *is the community truly being served and just what is the philosophy of a newsroom?* Check the fourth Terrible Truth. The time given to stories actually sought out by the news department is, unfortunately, anemic—compared to hard reality. Individual initiative by reporters is a great sounding term but dies in actual practice because almost every story, every idea, every issue…comes a knocking at the news room door. Reporters sitting down with the assignments editor or the news director actually happens sometimes but generally its to share a joke or a bratwurst sandwich, and not what stories might truly touch a viewer's nerve.

We live in a Newton*ian world*
of Einstein*ian physics*
ruled by Franken*stein logic*

David Russell

In a society that values achievement, art, intelligence, and sound, rational solutions to known problems, we sometimes accept and even give our approval to the absurd while ignoring that, which would benefit us. Frankenstein logic doesn't always rule us but does offer enough influence to defy understanding of why we do the things we do. It is really about the only way to explain the motives and actions of TV viewers who are used as pawns, much like those who are maneuvered and persuaded to buy shampoo or automobiles by the Houdinis of marketing. As has already been pointed out, the anchor is the major reason many viewers will watch a particular station. But this doesn't account for the slide in the number of viewers for several years before leveling out—but not increasing—in the beginning of the new century. Stations are recognizing they have to scramble to build an audience with something other than the powerful personality of an anchor. So marketing departments and news consultants, using surveys about what does and doesn't work to hold someone's attention, stoke the fires of a viewer's more prurient nature.

If the personal magnetism of the anchorman or woman of a station's nearest competitor could somehow be neutralized, there will be a greater chance to build or increase a following. Or if it already has an anchor that radiates sunshine in the dead of night, there must be a way to keep and enhance the audience it already owns. TV stations know they can't rest on their laurels, even if the male anchor is a Greek God or the female anchor is beauty and brains personified. There is always change in the wind and the smart stations must always be working on the foundation of a solid news department as well as nourishing a budding Brian Williams, Walter Cronkite or even a Dick Nourse. If the local stations have learned nothing else in fifty odd years of broadcasting the news …it is that nothing is forever. Within a period of two years, after a decade or more of no change, NBC, CBS and ABC lost their anchors for three different reasons. Local stations are just as vulnerable. All have to be ready for change.

Harmony is seldom the lead story.
Silas Bent

As mentioned, the cornerstone of a nightly newscast is sometimes a dizzying array of people being shot, robbed, stabbed, injured or being chased—as well as journalists reporting dastardly deeds live from the scene, sometimes—actually preferring—standing against a stiff wind or thundershower. The viewers repulsed and saddened by the stories, still eats'em up.

There was a period of time when television news operations tried to be more sophisticated about their stories and led their newscasts with something important or of high interest to the viewer. But as technology and more money became available and the drive to increase the ratings became paramount, news consultants discovered that underneath all that desire to be well informed, a measureable chunk of the viewers really possessed a heart more in tune to the pulse of a flashing red light, as long as it wasn't flashing on his front lawn. Apparently it is just the bedtime snack folks out there in TV land love before calling it a day.

For the station, there is always the sweet smell of success if it is the first on the scene and finds people running amuck and the police trying to hold back the curious, giving comfort to the victim(s) while corralling witnesses, if not the perpetrator himself, all against the backdrop of the ubiquitous flashing red lights. Of course, the stations can't always be so lucky. Most of the time the action isn't so hot and the story may have happened one to five hours earlier in the day and the police are just mopping up. So the reporter and producer on the scene do the next best thing. They make it look like it just happened, interjecting as much excitement as possible with sound bites of eyewitnesses or someone who *thinks* they know what happened and the reporter starting and ending his report live on-camera at the scene. Of course the report is more effective if it is raining and the reporter has to hold an umbrella *and* a mike. The stations do about anything they can to bring immediacy to the story, short of bringing along their own set of portable set of flashing red lights. If it's a non-story they make it look like the scoop of the day. But in fairness, some, and I mean only *some*, stories do have enough elements to them to warrant on-the-scene coverage, maybe not as a lead story and certainly not with the number of minutes it is given. It could be anything from a daring robbery to a spectacular crash to a suspected murder with a killer on the loose. Though reasonably rare, it's enough to bolster an excuse given by the station to justify why they do what they do.

If it is a lead story, the stations then have the task of following it up with another story with some of the same elements, like a meaningless car wreck or some other non-story but with a visual to hold a viewer's interest. It's called the "Hook and Hold" approach. It doesn't take a doctor of psychology to explain the concept. *Hook* a viewer with a feast for the eyes and maybe you'll *hold* him through the whole newscast. The problem is…this same 'hook and hold' idea is also practiced by all the stations in a market at the same time. Each newscast tries to make it seem like *they* have the big story of the night, complete with a reporter live on the scene, the night sky and, more often than not, those damnable flashing red lights in the background. The end result of all this jockeying around is to add new layers to the definition of news and totally confuse the viewers about what is and what isn't true journalism, if they really gave a damn in the first place.

Interestingly, after all the fuss over the lead stories on the ten o' clock news one would think the newspapers the next morning would be buzzing about the "big" stories of the day and night before. The viewer who becomes a reader the next morning anxiously opens the paper and rarely, only rarely, finds mention of any one of the stories that were so important the night before on television. And if it is there, it will likely be on the back page somewhere. The North County Times, a newspaper in San Diego, saves its back page for what it calls the lurid and mundane stuff, most of which were probably lead stories the night before on the area's television stations.

> *Journalists who say they give the public what it wants*
> *begin by underestimating public taste*
> *and end by corrupting it.*
> Pilkington Report

Somehow this idea of people loving the idea of the flashing red lights, and all that goes with it, is shoved down the throat of journalists by consultants. It is not a compliment to the viewers or management of the station…and it is offensive to a group of men and women who like to consider themselves as legitimate members of the Fourth Estate. The fact that viewers tolerate it day after day is an insult to their intelligence. And the stations should remember that 50% of the potential viewers have elected not to watch and do something else instead of subjecting themselves to all the fireworks off the top of the news. Does this single fact really register with management? Underestimating the public taste is one thing but to continue to feed the beast is another. But then, *whatever* adjustments recommended by the critics and viewers will likely fall on deaf ears. Management, promotion, consultants, reporters and producers will continue on their merry way, currying favor with that part of the potential viewers that still buy into the latest concepts and gimmicks to hold an audience. They seem oblivious to the fact they are maintaining the road that leads to total corruption of public taste.

For now, another interesting dimension to this 'hook and hold' tool is that the four major stations in the Salt Lake City market, for instance, all do their 'live' reports right off the top of the newscast. One would think they were all bird-dogging the same stories. Right? Wrong! Only rarely do they lead their newscasts with the same information or same characters. The common denominator among them is, of course, the reporter "live" against a night time sky, someone being interviewed that has something to say, the words *breaking news* titled across the screen, and probably some flashing red lights thrown in for good measure. Unfair to the viewer? Probably…but this is the competitive spirit at work.

Surveys have found that a reporter *"live on the scene"* gives the story more credibility and thus more interest. This is all well and good except for those lead stories with little or no substance, which is most of the time. But frankly, the viewer has an impossible time discerning what is substantive and what is not. It's all about rivalry with the other stations, of being top dog in the dog pound.

While local TV stations fiercely compete with one another, none fear local newspapers. One thing that the electronic media has done well is carve out its own niche for news. Of course, they cover a lot of the same stuff but competing with the print media is comparing carrots to coconuts. While both are trying to describe what has been happening around their coverage area, there is an almost entirely dissimilar idea about the choice of subject material. The papers' front page and the TV stations' lead stories are nowhere close to being the same. Television has been nurturing the same old notion for a couple of decades, *'if it bleeds, it leads.'* It is now refined with the *'hook and hold'* model, yet in its promotion tries to convince its audience that it is out there looking out for the viewer's social, financial, emotional, physical and cultural welfare. And it will do just that if there is enough room left in the newscast after all those flashing red lights, and man's inhumanity to man.

If you saw a man drowning and you could either save him
or photograph the event, what kind of film would you use?

Unknown

This rather cynical quote has more than a sliver of truth to it. Photogs, newspaper and TV types, love to get that once in a lifetime shot, even if someone has to die for it. However, never let it be said that a photographer hasn't thrown down his camera and run to aid a potential victim…but also never let it be said that he *has* thrown down his camera when he knows there is nothing he can do to save someone. Quite the contrary. He will grind away until the deed is done and someone is dead or badly injured. You've heard anchormen say things like…*"The following video is very graphic. You may not want your kids to see it."* It is what cameramen and women do. Airing or printing it is what editors do. Watching it is what viewers do. It's the nature of the beast. So much the better if there is a flashing red light in the picture.

News—covering it, writing about it, photographing it, and airing it is not for the faint-of-heart. When the event has been aired there are stations that feel inclined to put on another hat and act as a public servant and alert the public to possible danger or let people know of a need for further information to help the police locate a perpetrator. This type of information is not considered journalism per se but more like a public service announcement.

Some declarations are obvious and needed but others are not necessarily required within the body of a newscast. It comes dangerously close to an editorial stance, which is forbidden in newscasts where neutrality is a watchword. There is an additional feature to the idea of public service within the newscast and that is when the reporter becomes an instructor. A story may become a springboard to a lesson in how to perform a particular function or to prevent this or that from happening. One story dealt with a small child trying to climb on top of a dresser, thereby shifting the balance of the dresser itself and toppling a small television set on top of the dresser, onto the child, causing serious injury. The reporter saw an opportunity to present the public service of showing how this can be prevented, however obvious it might seem. She went to a hardware store and interviewed the manager and together they showed how a bracket could be attached to the TV set and then be secured while still sitting on the dresser. The lesson took more time in the newscast than the original story.

My favorite was a reporter who was trying to provide tips to viewers how to cut down on the possibility of being robbed. It focused on one key element; keep your doors locked. She interviewed a guy who left his garage door open and had his golf clubs stolen. Duh! And another lost his bicycle when he left it laying on the front lawn overnight. Double Duh! She admonished the viewers to keep things locked up. Just how stupid does she think her viewers are anyway? This type of journalism has no place in the newscast. News is hard enough to define but admonishments to the viewer, via a visual lesson, are sometimes as obvious as the likelihood of getting wet if you stand in the rain. One local station does it so often it is obvious that consultants have urged the news department to get close to its viewers with lessons in living, giving them something to relate and respond to. These "lessons" are obviously a part of their overall strategy to bring in the viewers. Good luck. As it is, there is barely enough time now for all the news. Rarely, if ever, does the newspaper have the space, time or desire to print such stories, let alone pause to teach a lesson to its readers. If it does, it sells the space.

> Carmella Soprano: *You made a fool of yourself on National f_____ television.*
> Anthony Soprano: *I didn't even say that s___! They totally misquoted me.*
> Carmella Soprano: *Of course they did,*
> **That's what they do!**
>
> HBO—the Sopranos 2006

TV news puts on its best Rodney Dangerfield face when bemoaning its reputation. *I don't get no respect from the viewers*…or even from other shows on TV. If the truth be told, TV news hasn't *got any respect* since John Cameron Swasey first went on the air in the 1940's. Respect is hard to come by in whatever industry one is in…and if it happens to be in journalism, the road is a particularly tough one, with holes big enough to swallow a viewer's natural gullibility.

Bluntly, TV journalists feel viewers don't have to like them if they will at least respect what they do. Newspaper reporters may edge out the electronic boys and girls in the *respect department* but for both it is a continuing uphill battle to gain total approval, whether print or broadcast. The one thing the introduction of radio and then television news has done is to spread the criticism to include *all* the media.

Before the idea of distributing information electronically was even a twinkle in Marconi's eye, newspapers took the bare brunt of heavy criticism. Tabloid and Yellow journalism have their roots that go deep into the early *1800's*. Thomas Jefferson was so frustrated with the newspapers of his day that he said; *advertisements...contain the only truths to be relied on in a newspaper.* Now newspapers have companions to share the blame.

No one doubts the immediacy TV news can bring to the viewing public. Newspapers may be able to give you every possible detail but it can't rival television in visual description and time frames. Those are distinct benefits and they are what TV news does particularly well, even though a high percentage of the stories die a sudden death once the reporter signs off on them. In short, news on TV is 'forgettable.' Two minutes later the viewer has only a scant recollection of the story.

> *I have come to the feeling about news on television*
> *the way I do about hamburgers.*
> *I eat a lot of hamburgers*
> *and don't remember a single one of them.*
>
> John Barrow

The real contradiction is that too many people lazily depend almost exclusively on television for their news, and like the hamburger, barely remember any of the stories. Even electronic journalists want an audience to be fully informed about their community...and TV falls depressingly short. In fact, surveys report 65 to 70% of the population allows television to be the dominant force of news in their lives. This statistic has been challenged by reputable firms, but even the newspaper industry hasn't made much of a fuss about it.

It's no secret that stations desperately try to make viewers dependent on them. Mainly this is done with a certain well-respected experienced, attractive anchor or with emphasize on a particular kind of coverage or any number of marketing tools that push that *dependence button* on a viewer. Maybe those flashing red lights have some hypnotic quality about them that turns a normally intelligent viewer into some kind of automaton.

Be like your dog. Don't just sniff the world, roll around in it!
Host, TV's The Planet's Funniest Animals

Sniffing is what journalists do. But that's only the beginning. They do like to roll around in their stories as well. Good journalists get their hands dirty, but that's what happens when you turn over every rock in the road. And not to let all that effort go to waste, the TV station does all it can to let everyone know the results of all that hard work. Almost every function performed by a TV station is designed to somehow increase the audience size and specifically, to make viewers dependent on that station's newscasts. Today, a news operation uses every imaginable idea to bring that dependence to fruition…everything from snappy promotions, paying outrageous sums of money to get the most appealing people, using every piece of new and splashy piece of equipment, the use of clever production techniques, shooting interesting, funny, unique and striking video and pulling out every gimmick in its bag of tricks.

They put that big pile of oats we discussed in the first *Terrible Truth* in the middle of the clearing every day and watched the viewers lap it up. But oats as a steady diet, if you asked a seasoned farmer, will ultimately give hogs diarrhea and limit their capacity to breed little hogs. They need supplemental nourishment. So do TV viewers. And so do those who are responsible for gathering and preparing the daily events for presentation. For too long and probably for a whole lot longer, the viewers are going to have to live on that daily pile of oats. One day, either the viewers or the news departments are going to wake up and realize just how nutritionally unbalanced those oats really are. Thankfully, there are some movements being made by journalists to make this less of a terrible truth.

Those who practice the art or raw skill of the journalistic profession are not your nine to fivers, or those who watch but don't see, or are faint of heart. Journalists are second cousins to a curious cat, a mother-in-law to a new groom and a chilly breeze to a public official. They don't miss much and are alert to everything around them. They don't care who wins the game but *how* it was played. They don't care who wins an election, only the *character and conduct* of the candidates—the shoddier the better. They can perform the most incredible public service to the community yet have no problem skinning someone alive for the pure pleasure of it. To be a journalist in every sense is not something that just comes out of the blue. You don't suddenly acquire the fascinating list of skills needed to be a good one.

Wanting to be a journalist begins long before the thought of being one even enters your head. Or at least that is the way it is suppose to go. There's something in every good reporter that pushes him or her to find a way to be set apart from the others or at the very least, be recognized for a talent that transcends the day-to-day mediocrity that is produced on the evening newscasts. The good ones never give up and they push until their insides hurt.

Tom Hanks: Don't tell me you're quitting. I thought you were a ball player.
Gina Davis: It's only a game.
Tom Hanks: Baseball is inside you.
Gina Davis: It just got too hard.
Tom Hanks: It's suppose to be hard. If it wasn't hard, everyone would be doing it. It's the hard that makes it great.

Scene from "A League of Their Own."

Hanks could have been talking about journalism. The profession isn't easy, by any standard of measurement. When it is done right, it *is* hard! It is also sleepless nights, ungodly hours, brick walls and little reward. The good ones stick with it, and excel. One I know well is Martha Raddatz. Her mother was my assistant and urged me to talk with her after a bad experience at a previous station. At the time she was a photographer but carried a degree in journalism. I hired her as a photographer above advice from the newsroom. Some felt she was trouble. Being aggressive was more the case. She wanted equal status because she felt she was every inch the journalist she was hired to be. I noticed right away that the reporters to whom she had been assigned to shoot film/tape were handing in better stories than before.

As it turned out…Martha not only shot their tape but gave great suggestions in how to cover the story. When a reporter slot opened up, I put her in it…and both of us never looked back. She had all the marbles to be a great one. Almost immediately, she stood out from the rest. Eventually she moved to Boston where she tore up the market and garnered a few Emmys…and ultimately to ABC news where she became one of the more valued correspondents. I would like to say I taught her everything she knows. Yah, like I helped Frank Lloyd Wright design The Guggenheim.

In absolute truth, I only opened a door for Martha. She had a natural instinct about journalism, its importance and its needs. She had a drive that no one in town could match. She was absolutely unrelenting when digging out a story and a fearless approach to put it into a workable form for broadcast.

Martha's numerous visits to Iraq during the war testify to her skill and courage. But she also had something else—an uncompromising attitude in her profession. There was never any doubt in her mind that she wasn't doing the thing she was cut out to do. She has a professional focus, whether local, national or international. She gives more than others were willing to give. She knows more because she schools herself with every side of a story. She does more than anyone else to make sure the story is fair and fully covered. She is the standard bearer of all men and women who desire to tackle this profession. She has been the Chief White House Correspondent for ABC News, later the Pentagon Correspondent and at this writing, she is the Senior Foreign Affairs Correspondent for ABC News…and the President of the United States calls her by her first name.

Obviously, I am proud of Martha but can only take a very small amount of credit in her rise to the network level. Along the way, she encountered many others—managers, fellow colleagues, correspondences of depth and tenure— who contributed to her success, if nothing more than opening more doors. It was her touchstones of ambition, skill and readiness that moved her to that next step, while the rest of us on the local level did the best we could with what brainpower we possessed to inch ahead day by day. For me, my initial disadvantage was one of being so terribly naïve, so progress was bound to be slow, but I had the good fortune to meet and work with people of quality who taught me the true meaning of professionalism. Others, with a lot more talent than me, weren't so lucky and never reached their potential.

My landing at KSL was pure coincidence…and I naturally assumed all managers on that level were men and women of quality, honor, smarts, benevolence and balance. Being from a Montana farm and a very small town I didn't have a lot of exposure to the "real world" of business and zero experience and knowledge in broadcasting.

I obviously thought every company of stature would have a superb manager. KSL Radio had Joe Kjar at the helm. To this day, after working and watching many others from a front row seat and dealing with company heads and captains of industry, I have never encountered another Joe Kjar.

For me personally, I started at the top and didn't know it. I can't explain why I had the unmitigated, blind good luck to stumble into a manager of his quality right out of the chute. The bar was already on the top rung, standards of ethics and work discipline were well defined, and there was no excuse for me not knowing the meaning and demonstration of excellence on all levels. The chances of finding a Joe Kjar down the line would have been slim to none.

As I moved into a rapidly developing TV news department, my luck held fast and I was further nurtured by the news director, Ted Capener, who demonstrated patience, guidance and a responsibility to the viewer. Both men were eventually voted into the state's Broadcast Hall of Fame. I spent the rest of my career trying to live up to their standard, a task at which I've fallen short more times than I care to admit…but for them, found the ride much more pleasurable than I could ever have imagined.

> *The first step is to understand that TV news*
> *is just a delivery system for ads.*
> *A show is a success if the people who watched it*
> *go and buy the products that were advertised during the commercials.*
>
> Dean Batali
> TV writer

The secret is out. We're not providers. We're salesmen. We're selling cars, deodorants, clothes, etc. etc. At least that's how a TV sales department and much of management view the news department. They may challenge this accusation…and if they do, it's the height of hypocrisy. TV news *is* a business, and the boys and girls in the news department sometimes forget that elementary fact.

Christine Amanpour, a controversial network correspondent, in one of her better moments, did put it in proper perspective when she declared, *"Yes, we are running businesses and yes we understand and accept that ...but surely there must be a level beyond which profit from news is simply indecent."*

Some corporations try not to be so obvious about their 'indecent profits' but make no apology for it. Money is, after all, the fuel to keep the motor running but TV News is one of the very few industries where the product walks and talks and, if necessary, crawls on its belly across a foreign battle field. This product is not like a car that will get you from point A to point B, or a box of soap that will clean your clothes or the movies & music where you can take them home and put them on the shelf and endlessly play them for enjoyment. We're talking about human beings who ingratiate themselves before your very eyes and keep you around long enough for the commercial to convince you to buy whatever is being sold. They like to think they are trying to win your trust and provide information that is important to your life, to help you make decisions, to make you aware of all the stumbling blocks to avoid, to help make you a more interesting and informed person. But let's get down and dirty about this whole management/news business.

While we purists like to think that local TV news is an opportunity to inform a needy audience; TV management has a whole different take. They recognize some key points in their programming schedules; news programs make money while at the same time, the audience is purported to be getting smaller. Robert A. Papper, professor of Telecommunications at Ball State University and author of a major examination of media use, says that the proliferation of news programs—morning, noon, afternoon, late afternoon, early evening and late evening—is not about *audience*, it's about *money*. Over 40 percent of revenue comes from local news. It's a huge number for any station to replace if they are contemplating other types of programming. Plus, as Papper says*, there are commercial buys that only go to stations that run news. No news, no buy.* Certainly, the stations want a larger audience but won't gamble by cutting back on news programming. *Management knows*, continues Papper, that the viewers also *get information from other less traditional broadcast and cable sources that not everyone even agrees is real news. Outrageous. And if more than six people ever figure out what TiVo is, the industry could really be in trouble.*

Papper's findings are reinforced by the annual report on American journalism that says...*newsrooms have felt a decade of intensifying demands to find more 'revenue opportunities.' Even the impetus to create new hours of news programming, in part, is a function of looking for more revenue.* So the viewers don't want to delude themselves into thinking that all those news programs are there to further enlighten them about their world and community. It's about money, which is generally fine because we all know that the station(s) must make enough to cover expenses, but some of the tripe they produce for those earlier programs is embarrassing to the industry.

In the final analysis, for the viewer and the journalist, it isn't always the information that is being spilled out, it's whether you like and trust the man or woman who is *presenting* the information...and there are people out there who are getting rich trying to find out who you *do* like...and why.

Whether it is a journalist's skill or looks or something they say or the *way* they say it...there has to be a system to determine just how effective they are, even if it means some bloodletting when the viewers are less than enthusiastic about them. Enter the rating system! Performance is measured all year long, but twice a year, the companies who do the measuring really get serious.

Fundamentally, the rating system is a measurement of who and how many are watching *who* and *what*, and sometimes *why*. Inside the news room, the rating systems can determine whether careers are going up or down, whether salary raises are going to be given out or shelved, whether formats will stay the same, whether news directors can or should get their résumés in order.

Big, heavy books can be written explaining the whole rating structure. In TV news, the ratings system is the most ominous cloud to hang over a newsroom, and over the anchor people in particular. The big rating periods are in the spring and fall. Most attention is given the latter because of the introduction of the new fall programs and the results are announced just before Christmas. Some sadistic bastard who puts ice down an old lady's dress must have thought that one up. A good many station managers and news directors have had their holidays ruined by a poor showing. One of the reasons they are so important has nothing to do with the pride of being number one. It may be to the newsroom, but additional rating points mean additional dollars in the till.

As mentioned, 40% to 45% of a station's revenue is generated by the news programs. A jump of a single rating point can mean hundreds of thousands of dollars...the difference between being number one and number two in a medium size market is in excess of millions of dollars a year in earnings. So when a TV news presentation slips in ratings, it becomes more than just a problem to the newsroom. The sales department and other levels of management start to grind their teeth, bite their fingernails, second guess, and commence to commission more polls to determine what's going on. No matter how good you may have been, for how long, if you don't win the rating wars, or at least hold your own or show improvement, loyalty and good journalism are not mentioned in the same breath. It's a game of economics, and if a sizeable portion of the audience doesn't like your face or your manner, it could mean goodbye, even if you write like Tolstoy, read like Laurence Oliver, and look like Brad Pitt. It's all about the ratings!

Several times a year a newsroom has to gear up for presentation of their best stuff, saved up specifically for the rating period. It's great for the viewers but intense pressure for the producers and reporters. They may not enjoy the process but they do like the numbers, if things go their way. The most important rating period is during the introduction of the network's new fall programs. It is a time when an audience will be exposed to exposés, hot feature stories, stories of high interest that run over a period of several days, exclusive investigative pieces, production techniques and heavy promotion. As stated, it's all a numbers game. In fact, it is *always* a numbers game. How many people and dollars can a station entice through the archway. The stories and news coverage is only a means to an end ($$$).

Improved rating points give promotion directors a temporary euphoria until the next rating period, which may then give them heartburn. Much of the promotion of a news department is predicated on ratings. Promoting a number three station in a three station market is akin to trying to convince viewers that hamburger tastes like filet mignon. Generally speaking, all stations cover essentially the same stories with their own independent features designed to entertain and inform. It's the anchors who are also ruthlessly scrutinized. Unless an anchor is entrenched with many years in the same seat…ratings can be a death knell. As a result, anchors are among the most insecure people on earth, and for good reason. Is it said that when logic is applied to advertising and marketing, the public and the whole process are in trouble. The same is true when people are asked what station they are watching or like to watch at particular times of the day. Like advertising they are reacting from some visceral level that most of the time defies logic. It is particularly true when someone is asked why they prefer this or that newscast. And when you throw in some half truths like *TV news does not stick to the bones* or *memories are short,* the ratings take on a life of their own and act as a barometer of the culture as well as individual habits. Most frustrating of all has nothing to do with the news itself but the program preceding the news. If it has a low rating or is anathema to the viewer, he is more apt to change the channel to watch his favorite news program. If it is a popular program, viewers are more likely to just stay with the same channel for the news.

If you watch only television news and become dependent on it, as so many say you are, will you—like those boar hogs mentioned earlier…be trapped? There is already a mountain of evidence that says you are already lassoed, pinned and tied, and yet, you can't remember more than a third of what you saw and heard. And there are surveys to prove it.

A marketing class at the University of Utah once tested viewers of a TV newscast of the previous evening, and found only 10% of the information was remembered. Of course, the more dramatic the news, the higher the recall. But ninety percent of news of the day is filled with rather ordinary items of interest. And because there is an abundance of ordinary news, TV news departments try to milk the big story for everything its worth. And too many times, it's not worth very much, but they try to spiffy it up as much as possible and generally spend twice the time it deserves.

There *is* something to say about the *printed* word. It never goes away. It's there for reference, for examination, analysis and criticism. But the *spoken* word is not only hard to remember, it is generally remembered wrong. The spoken word also demands attention. If you didn't hear it all the first time you can't rewind the anchorman/woman for a rerun. If you are concerned or particularly interested in the anchor's suit, dress, hairstyle, voice, smile, eyes, makeup…or are distracted by your kid jumping up and down on your lap, then you may miss a critical word or two or three in the story that could dilute its impact, not to mention some salient facts. If those young, rookie politicians who get roasted from time to time on TV would remember this, they'd sleep much better. They think that all the viewers in the world probably heard what exactly was said and will remember it forever. The seasoned politicians shrug it off.

What people do remember is the person trying to refute what was said by making a big stink about it.

About a decade or so ago, a magazine called The New Nation, with a circulation of *about 40*, published results of a straw survey it had taken on the intelligent quotient of members of the U. S. Senate. A Southern senator was listed at the bottom. Instead of ignoring the slipshod survey—read only by a very few and disregarded by major publications—the senator called a news conference to deny it. In the words of columnist, Art Buchwald, *this truly made him the dumbest senator in the U. S. Senate.*

What TV news departments can do very well is cover an important story from several angles. For example, if the station carries a story about a prominent person dying of a rare case of tuberculosis, the news department may follow it up with a story on a history of the disease, its different dimensions, etc. Likely, more time would be spent on the follow up story then was spent on the person who died from it. Most of these stories are not only interesting but vital to a viewer's information bank.

As a youngster in Saco, movies were an integral part of our daily life. We may have had four bars and three grocery stores in a town of 400 but we also had the Gem Theater. The cost was just nine cents. My favorite movies were Westerns…and my hero was Roy Rogers. That's right, King of the Cowboys, Roy Rogers.

Riding a horse like no man alive was good old Roy. He could ride like the wind when he wasn't singing a song or knocking some guy senseless. I tolerated the singing, loved the fighting but what I liked best was to see him saddle up Trigger and chase the bad guys across the screen. Even as I got older I never lost my devotion to Roy. His museum in Victorville, Ca. was always a must stop for me. And then, as luck and the Gods of Western movies would have it…I got to meet the man himself. He was in Salt Lake City for some unannounced promotional stopover of his Roy Rogers restaurants.

I learned that Roy was staying at a local hotel and so I lost no time in putting myself on the schedule board to do an interview. I called his room and scheduled an appointment through his assistant. I had interviewed men and women of all stripes but somehow talking with Roy was one of life's treasured moments. Seeing him in-person for the first time was an incredible experience. Words can't describe my feelings.

Roy and I sat down in a comfortable suite and straight away I became very comfortable with him. He was gracious and very accommodating. I, of course, blabbered about my youth and my love of his Westerns. The interview, while never being sealed in a time capsule, went well. At the conclusion I asked what his schedule was for the rest of the day. He said he'd be flying out of town later in the afternoon but first had to visit the Roy Rogers restaurant in an area of town called Sugar House and would be leaving for the place in a matter of minutes. I asked if the restaurant knew he was on his way and he said no. He said it was much more fun to surprise the people. We warmly shook hands and I told him not to be surprised if he saw me there. He said that would be fine but not to tell anyone.

I left for the restaurant immediately, ordered a Dr. Pepper and took a seat. Ten minutes later Roy and an associate arrived. When he walked in, he was dressed to the nines, and by pure coincidence just happened to stand next to a Roy Rogers life sized placard. There were about five or six booths filled and the patrons all seem to see him at the same time and immediately filled the room with applause. The staff of the restaurant was totally caught by surprise but before meeting them Roy walked to each booth and shook everyone's hand. When he got to me he leaned over and quietly said, "How am I doing?" I shook his hand again and said, "*Just like the Roy I've always known.*" He smiled and told me it was an honor to meet me, then went behind the counter and warmly greeted a very surprised but grateful staff.

It was an honor to meet me? Believe me, Roy, the honor was all mine.

I've interviewed a few Presidents, corporate giants, a slew of celebrities but nothing rivaled that afternoon. Roy was my hero then and in my dreams, still is. Being a journalist does have its moments…and they don't always have to be investigating corruption or putting someone on the spot. It is helping people make decisions, illuminating different dimensions of the community, warning them of shoddy practices and products, providing information to enlighten, entertain and expose…and then there are times of, unadulterated, enchanting, unimaginable pleasure. The sound bite I used on the news that night was certainly not news in the purest sense but did hold its own with the rest of the stories. It wasn't about issues or politics or religion or something that happened that day or something that affected our lives. Rather, it was a few words from a man who was living his life well, with solid moral values, with a happy, well adjusted family, while bringing joy to millions of people over the years. He made us remember the way it was and what we may have forgotten. At the very least he brought a smile to our collective face. We were reminded that once upon a time there was a good man out there who helped make us better with his beliefs, with his examples, and the movies he made. And, even now in our memories, for some of us, Roy could still out-shoot, out-ride, out-fight and out-sing anyone West of the Pecos. With Roy, I felt I had, for a moment, grasped the brass ring. In this business, there has never been a moment before or since, to match it.

9.
An ordinary picture
takes precedence
over the most profoundly written word.

He gave her a look you could have poured on a waffle.
Ring Lardner

Ah…you can just about see in your mind's eye, the face of a man who found the fair damsel of his dreams. And a woman reading the same words would love to have her man look at her in the same way. Waffles would never taste the same again for either of them.

Some words, appropriately arranged in a sentence, can take the place of a superb picture, to a point where you can not only see what is being described but feel as well. Or, there can be words used to describe an idea where pictures would only interfere. Even some historic events are better left to those consummate wordsmiths of the human condition. Lincoln is an obvious candidate. Listening to Edward R. Murrow, in the late 1930's, describe a blitzkrieg over London while broadcasting from a rooftop for network radio, created images in the mind that have never faded away.

Through the ages, in reporting the news, words painted pictures in our mind's eye that educate, fascinate and stir our imaginations. And we loved it. But now, we have real pictures to accompany those words…and it's hard to tell if we're any better for it. No one denies the power of a visual reference to what is being described, but, sadly, pictures—no matter how mediocre—permeate our culture, leaving us with images that only tell *part* of the story. In the end there has to be verbal descriptions of events as well. After all, words are still the meat and potatoes of a reporter's job. If a reporter is not up to the task, in Harry's Reasoner's own words—as we have stated before—*the viewer will become vaguely uncomfortable and turn away.*   Stations will also put cover video of meaningless images that would conceal a reporter's *in*-ability to adequately describe the finer points of a story. At the same time, because of the short period of time allotted the story, reporters do use the video to carry some of the reporting duties.

Probably more than most, Stan Freiberg was a man who knew how to use words to create lasting images in our mind's eye. In a 30 second radio spot, he once presided over the job of turning Lake Michigan into a huge cup of hot chocolate with whip cream being thickly layered on top…and a plane flying overhead, dropping a huge cherry in the middle of it all. He used all the sound effects to go along with his play by play and when it was over, you didn't doubt that there existed a gigantic cup of hot chocolate, complete with whip cream, topped with a cherry. In your head you could not only see but smell and taste all the ingredients. Words made the impossible, possible.

And then there are local TV newscasts where words are a mere addendum to the pictures being broadcast. An old argument will creep in whenever you spend too much time praising the beauty of words and their necessity in fleshing out details of a story, any story actually. Yes, *a picture can be worth a thousand words*, depending on the time and place they are used. We can't all put together 272 words like old Abe to change the course of history, but we can be selective with our choice of words that will also enhance the video and provide clarity and meaning to the story. People use to travel a hundred miles by horse and buggy to hear a speaker who painted pictures with nothing but words. Today, it is easy for people to feel *'vaguely uncomfortable'* when the writing lacks cohesion and creativity…and then is compounded when the reporter relies on his video to carry him through.

We sometimes forget the public's intelligence. We had a running philosophy in the news room that we tried to make ourselves believe was true, even though we were barely conscious of it when producing our stories*: give the people accurate, understandable information to let them know what is going on in their community and world…and maybe, just maybe, they will be better equipped to make decisions in their lives that make sense.* A little over the top maybe, but who knows, at times, we may have done just that.

The right visual can move a grown man to tears, make his heart soar, or hide his head in shame. One visual in particular probably did all three in Rome where, in 1968, the Utah delegation was making a bid for the 1980 Winter Olympics, long before it actually won the privilege. The U. S. Committee picked Salt Lake City to represent the country, knowing the chance of winning the bid was akin to winning the lottery without buying a ticket. But the Utah group dutifully made the trip to Rome where all the bidding countries had assembled. The Utah committee was small in size: a Utah National Guard General, a Salt

Lake City Commissioner, a couple of others…and the three SLC local TV News Directors without their reporters and photographers. Local coverage would be slight, if at all. The low expectation of winning was hardly worth the price of a plane ticket.

To be gracious hosts for the bidding process the Italian government arranged for tours of various kinds for the nations involved. Utah was given the privilege of touring Vatican City and its crown jewel, the Sistine Chapel. The group was further given the honor of having a full-fledged English speaking Cardinal conduct the tour.

Eventually, the circuit found its way into the venerable Chapel. As any tourist knows who has visited the small but magnificent edifice, it is very crowded and noisy. But on this particular day, being Thursday and the only day of the week when the Chapel was closed, the Utahans, by a special dispensation, stepped into a pristine environment, empty and silent, as though the artist himself had prepared the way. Nearly all admitted it was a spiritual experience. The Cardinal quietly explained a few little known points of interest about Michelangelo's painting on the Chapel ceiling and then subtlety stepped away a few steps from the group to allow them to drink in one of the world's greatest artistic achievements. For nearly a whole minute, there was not the hint of a sound of any kind. Until! The Salt Lake County Commissioner who was a former truck driver for the Utah Copper Corporation and who narrowly won his elected spot on the commission was the first to speak in an unkindly loud voice the words that are still bouncing off the Chapel walls…*I'll kiss your ass if that ain't sumthin.*

Utah did not win the bid to host the 1980 Winter Olympics.

There is no arguing the beauty, strength and effect of a great picture or film that captures a moving moment, be it tragic, gratifying or simply funny. Many times, words are just not necessary. The image of the American flag being raised on Mt. Surabachi on Iwo Jima will forever be burned in our minds and a vivid memory for the rest of photographer Art Rosenthal's life. He was defined by that single picture, even though it wasn't posed and he had only a few seconds to click off only one shot to capture the event. Until the film was developed much later he wasn't sure he even had a picture and if he did, it was probably either out of focus or out of frame.

When his compatriots started congratulating him on the photograph, he thought the fuss was over a later picture he had taken of a group of marines around the flag's base. He had yet to see the actual flag raising shot. When the picture was put before him, even he was astonished at the statue-like image, flawlessly framed, in focus and a perfect representation of American strength and commitment.

Sadly, Bill Genaust, the man beside Rosenthal, taking 16mm movie footage wasn't able to see his developed film. A few days later he had stepped into a "secure" cave to have a smoke and suffered a gruesome death by a few of the enemy still hiding in the cave. Rosenthal, on the other hand, saw the 99th anniversary of his own life and worldwide acclaim.

Though I worked in television news almost exclusively with fascinating visual I never lost my love for the written…and especially, the *spoken* word. When words are properly connected it is almost impossible for the visual to compete with them. In my more mature years I have become enamored, almost fascinated with the impact that words can have on a given situation. For me, it started with a jolt when I was fourteen. I had a ringside seat to a life altering experience for about thirty kids.

While still in my teens I could see that race relations were one-sided and the separation between Blacks and Whites, especially, was evident anywhere you traveled. Some of the old disgusting practices prevailed but we accepted them as part of our lives. Even as teenagers we knew that it wasn't right but in our foolishness we shrugged our shoulders and stayed in our own corner. For a boy born and partly raised in Northeast Montana, Blacks were scarce as ski instructors in Kansas.

When I moved to North Richland, Washington we lived in one of the largest trailer towns in the country. It was broken up into a dozen blocks, numbered 100 to 1200…and each block into roads from A to M. There were paved streets and sidewalks, bathhouses on every street in every block and clotheslines for washing clothes. There were no doublewide trailers in those days. A 35 foot trailer was the length limit. During my fourteenth and fifteenth years I delivered newspapers to blocks 100 through 600, the latter exclusively for Blacks. I delivered roughly 80 papers throughout the six blocks and the truth is…the 600 block was my favorite. The residents were the most accommodating and always paid up when I made my monthly collection runs.

The cost for a month of papers, seven days a week, was $1.85. Still, it seemed to be an insurmountable amount to some of my subscribers and I would have to check with them 3 or 4 times every month to collect my fee. Not the 600 block. For some reason, the first time was the only time. It was from this backdrop of my early teenage years where I learned that mere words could have a life-altering effect.

One of my 600 block subscribers had a daughter a year older than me by the name of Missy who was always friendly and courteous, both at her home and in school. Because we lived in North Richland, all students had to ride the bus 10 miles to Columbia High School in Richland. That bus ride was a daily education. Every minute the bus was abuzz with adventures, gossip, who was doing what to whom, tales of wild escapades-sexual and otherwise, four letter words and a glossary of every fantasy and fact of life. For prepubescent boys it was a smorgasbord for those with a never-ending appetite.

Missy and her neighbor were the only two Black girls on the bus every morning and afternoon. They sat alone, talked only to themselves and rarely ever talked to others, as others rarely talked to them. In retrospect, it was a bad arrangement for everyone. But one morning something happened that affected all of us on the bus and one young man in particular. It was, as people are fond of saying, an *epiphany* in our lives. It was a rite of passage for most of us, for my attitude on a lot of things was changed forever. I just know I was never quite the same.

One of the students who rode the bus daily was a natural loudmouth but he was also a comedian to his friends, handsome to the girls and a step ahead of the rest of us on just about every level. He could also be very mean spirited, making fun of those of us who were still bordering on geekdom. Occasionally one of us would tell him to shut up, at which time he informed us he was ready to kick our ass anytime we were ready. He not only had the qualities I mentioned but he was also big for his age. No one seemed ready to challenge him.

As luck and life would have it, people of his breeding will eventually step over a line one too many times. One morning, while he was expounding on some subject of no particular interest except to himself, he made some vague reference to the Black girls sitting three rows ahead of him. To anyone's knowledge that is the last time he spoke above a conversational voice for the next 2 years of riding that bus. Like a shot, Missy whirled, put her knees on the seat and faced directly at her provocateur.   What followed was a lesson in retaliation and use of the King's English, the likes of which I or any other teenager had never encountered. For the next two minutes, in a voice that would melt cold hard steel; she used expletives that were more like lightning bolts than simple four letter words, while at the same time providing a brief, broad, dark history of her culture's difficult past and topped it off with the threat of how he would have to deal with her older brother and his friends if he *ever* talked to her again under *any* circumstance about *anything*. She described in minute detail of things that would happen to him that even in his wildest imagination he had never even considered or imagined, much less now believed could become a hard reality. And no one, I mean, no one on the bus, ever doubted for a moment that she meant every word. The one early lesson that was ingrained in all of us was never to take the power of the spoken word for granted. For the kids on the bus it was a day that will forever remain fresh in our minds. In total impact, Martin Luther King's *I Have a Dream* speech at the Washington, D.C Mall had nothing over on Missy's off-the-cuff response to an over-the-edge young man.

To say that everyone on the bus, including the loudmouth, was thunderstruck would be putting it mildly. For the next eight miles the bus driver must have thought he was driving an empty bus. There was not a sound or movement by anyone. 30 teenagers. Numbed. Paralyzed. Their vocal chords cut and their hearts removed. When the bus stopped, everyone filed off like walking mummies taken to a prison to begin serving a life sentence. They had nothing to say. It's probably true to think they didn't hear a thing in their first period class other than the ringing in their ears. I'm sure it took most of us the better part of the morning to once again solidly touch terra firma. Later in the day I passed Missy in the hall…and she winked.

That same night I was making my monthly collection rounds and as fate would have it, her parents were on my list. With some trepidation I knocked on the door and her father answered and, as usual, was friendly and accommodating, inviting me in to share his wife's freshly baked cookies. Missy was sitting on the couch and was equally pleasant. When I left she followed me outside and asked if everyone had survived the bus ride. I told her it was a ride we'd never forget. She said she was certainly aware of the impression she had made and felt that the loudmouth in question was long overdue to get his comeuppance. And then she said an incredible thing. Because my friends may have been offended by what she said, she would understand if I didn't say hello to her anymore on or off the bus. I suddenly felt ashamed of any resentment I may have felt toward any Black in my life. I told her that I would never do that and that it would be a privilege to always have her as a friend.

Amazingly, her popularity on the bus increased and nearly everyone started saying hello to her. And the loudmouth? No longer was he the noisiest guy on the bus or the boldest or the biggest braggart. He settled in and was more sincere to everyone. And then he did an equally amazing thing.

About a month later, collecting again at Missy's house, she again followed me outside and said, *"You'll never guess who came to my trailer last week."* After a slight pause, she said, "Who would you think would be the last person to come visit me?" I jokingly said, *"The bigmouth on the bus?"* She told me I was absolutely right. She said he came over and sincerely apologized for what he had said and that he was a changed person and would never again say anything stupid to her. I thought…wow, a brave gesture considering the threat that must have still been rattling around in his head of what would happen to him if he ever spoke to Missy ever again about *any* subject. They both survived it and I'm sure both are stronger and wiser than before. The one thing I do know is that I will never, ever take the power of the spoken word for granted. I just wish I knew where both of them are today. I would trade meeting several presidents, Ginger Rogers and case of Dr. Pepper to shake their hands.

> *The biggest danger to American journalism*
> *is not from commercial pressures or government regulations…*
> *but from a decline in public interest in current events.*
> Evan Cornog
> Publisher of Columbia Journalism Review

Cornog is probably very worried about the dangerous path we seem to be on, considering readers and viewers are steadily declining in numbers. He knows that roughly 70% of the population use TV for their major source of news. And he knows that most of the viewers of network news programs are over fifty years of age and that most local newscasts (with larger audiences than the network boys and girls) spend 50% of the allotted time talking about local crime and accidents. With all this data around the viewer, most must be ready to throw in the towel. Just how do you get people to be more interested in what is happening? Too many people don't watch the news because it is too negative and too many others don't take the time to read the newspaper, claiming they just don't have the time. The same is true for those who don't read weekly periodicals or watch weekly TV network news programs. It's too bad because the networks really do produce great stuff that does interest a large segment of the population. Most what they turn out, the viewer can either directly or indirectly relate. The local product, while expertly produced, doesn't often hit the viewer's hot button.

It is the local evening news that has the best chance of helping people raise their interest in current events. The opportunity certainly exists but as long as management worships the dollar, and electronic journalists are slaves to the ratings, and consultants are dictating the format, and viewers are being manipulated by marketing gurus, the Evan Cornogs of the world will continue to worry and his disciples will likely continue to worship at the alter of Gertrude Stein who was always looking for answers to the meaning of things that can't be changed….

There ain't no answer. There ain't goin' to be any answer.
There never has been an answer.
That's the answer!

Gertrude Stein
writer and curmudgeon

The old gal may be right. She could also have been talking about the continuing conflicts circling around Afghanistan or some crisis in Nevada. There are no answers for some of the dilemmas we face, in and out of journalism. If we call ourselves caring, dedicated and responsible individuals, we must at least acknowledge the public's declining interest in the daily news, other than some bull moose running loose on the freeway. Losing interest in current events has ramifications beyond a colorful graphic showing the waning numbers year after year. This is not a book to preach to the people in the television newsrooms for that would be futile. Management greed holds the trump card and as long as they are dependent on the advertising dollar, it will insist that the reporters still pay homage to that aforementioned damn old *If it bleeds, it leads* cliché that has built up over the years…and while most try to pretend they've never heard of it, others have subconsciously kept it as some invisible banner flying on the far wall of a newsroom.   This war cry is as much of an indictment of the public's thirst for blood as it is a slam at the media generally—journalism specifically and TV news precisely. The unmentioned, unwritten, and untidy acceptance and use of the catchphrase gives credence to the charge by journalism professors, newspaper editors, and selective viewers that stations believe that violence, in whatever form, is actually so ingrained in a viewing public that it desires and accepts it without hesitation. So current events, the stuff that truly affects you and your family's life, will either be buried in the newscast or ignored completely.

The more spectacular the car wreck, the higher its place in the newscast. And unless the King of Siam is killed in the car, the station's affiliated radio station wouldn't even mention it. Someday, someone is going to have to admit in some straightforward fashion or even some obscure way that *the visual dictates the flow of TV News*. There is nothing wrong with this as long as it is accepted both internally and externally and that true journalism has to lay down and play dead on a few (more than a few) stories. Call it show business, call it tabloid, call it cheap entertainment…but please don't call it journalism.

As mentioned, Webster says ***journalism*** *is the work of gathering, writing, editing, and publishing or disseminating* **_news_** *as through newspapers and magazines or by radio and television.* The key word in that definition is *news*. Again, **News,** says Webster, is… *new information about anything; information previously unknown; reports of recent happenings; any person or thing thought to merit special attention in such reports*.   Of course this doesn't substantially cover comments of opinion (editorials), investigative reporting, tabloid crap, advocacy treatments or examination of material behind a story, or feature reporting. There are always arguments available to both sides of the fence in either trying to define news or cross pollinating the different types of "news" to refute any charge to come their way, but the truth is they hardly have time to broadcast the dribble they do have. But there are those moments when some reporters step up to the plate and write profoundly well and put perfect images on the TV screen and actually make a difference. Not often…but often enough to keep the store open.

There is so much good in the worst of us,
and so much bad in the best of us,
that it hardly behooves any of us to talk about the rest of us.
Edward Wallis Hogh 1849-1925

It's what reporters do. They talk over the back fence with anyone who will listen. Hogh's quote from nearly a hundred years ago is probably still good advice today and has its disciples, mostly critics of all ages, on every corner. Reporters, the good ones, are busybodies and are going to talk to whoever they want, whenever they want, about anything they want. Generally, they want to find something that will roast someone's ass. Remember the My Lai incident in Viet Nam where U.S. soldiers killed innocent civilians, including children? Earlier in this book we quoted the respected and even venerated journalist Seymour Hersh; *Let me tell you about our profession. We are the meanest, nastiest bunch of petty, jealous, sons a bitches who ever lived. You think I wouldn't sell my mother for another My Lai?* Sweet guy. Journalists want the story and will step over bodies to get it. They may even shed a tear while covering it but they'll recover about ten times faster than any other witness. There is always the specter of a Pulitzer or Peabody prize riding on the frontal lobe of their brain. Frankly, local reporters are no different. The opportunities are just much fewer.

10.

**TV News loves to misbehave,
opting for controversy over substance,
creating an image,
and never letting a story die.**

I was young and foolish. It was really just a stupid act
by a stupid kid and then the media took over.
                                        Amy Fisher

I feel Amy Fisher's observation was one of the more interesting and revealing comments of the decade about the media. She was the sixteen year old mistress of married garage mechanic, Joey Buttafuoco. Claiming her lover told her to do it, Amy shot Mrs. Buttafuoco in the head. The wife survived but Amy served seven years in prison for her act. Amazingly, Buttafuoco stayed married to his wife for several more years and went on a tour of personal appearances. Buttafuoco was a name tailor-made for TV-print tabloid heaven. (In the beginning of his new late night talk show on CBS, David Letterman jokingly said he tried to work the Buttafuoco name into the title of his show.)

Fresh out of prison, in an interview with Katie Couric, Amy gave her great illuminating truth about electronic journalism. In summarizing her life she said there was her childhood, then Buttafuoco, then the attempted assassination, and then she said…*"…the media took over."* I doubt that there was hardly one person on the planet who didn't agree with her, including every journalist.

The comment by Amy generally went unnoticed, mainly because of the almost casual way it was presented. A few days later a writer for a local paper called it to my attention and I told him I did indeed hear it and agreed with Amy and whether she knew it or not, she had put her finger on this hidden button that is relentlessly pushed but rarely acknowledged. Too often a news gathering organization puts its own spin on a story. As objective as it tries to be there is always a little piece of the reporter's writing, the producer's aggression, the editor's scissors, the photographer's angle and the anchor's inflection, in almost every story; and the bigger the story, the bigger the piece. Worse, all the media will sometimes get into a lockstep about an event and gang up on both the public and the victim. What can the viewer, the listener, and the reader do except to buy into the story when the same conclusion is drawn by the three sides of the media triangle? The extent of the coverage can be so pervasive that it numbs the senses. What is sometimes lost in this frenzy of hype and sordid details are those background factors that contributed to Amy's behavior and the events leading up to her association with Joey. But, unfortunately, readers and viewers could care less. Most want it quick and dirty, straight up without the chaser. With or without all the information, no one gets off the hook. Indeed, when the media "takes over" there are no winners.

Nothing travels faster than the speed of light
with the possible exception of bad news.
Douglas Adams
The Hitchhiker's Guide to the Galaxy

Before television, it was the radio and the special edition of a newspaper that delivered the bad news with such efficiency. But that was then. On the morning of 9-11, 2001, millions of telephones rang all over the country and people heard these four words in their ears...*"Turn on your TV."* Whether major or minor, stories that tantalize or torment find television to be a willing accomplice. When a big story is unfolding, the only source the general population has is through the media, TV specifically. And when the story has those ingredients that touch our heart or gut, it doesn't take much for a reporter to rise to the occasion. He and his ilk can quickly take over a story and proceed to put their imprint on it.

Nine Eleven (9-11) aside, if a lazy viewer has no other source of reference for a story, he/she will likely take the reporter/producer/anchor at their word, not realizing that there are other sources to seek out, other facets of the event that will reveal more truths…but then that would be too much trouble. Too often the public forgets the *why* of an event and just go with what they have seen and heard from the reporter's point of view. Considering the story, this could be a dangerous precedent. People could and have developed a mindset about someone's guilt or innocence without the full due process of law. Even if someone *is* found guilty, sentenced and eventually released, the media is always quick to remind everyone of the crime(s). As long as there is any blood left to squeeze out of a story a news organization will do everything under its power to drain the body of any vital fluids.

In a country that believes in second chances there is an industry that is anxious to increase the odds of eliminating that chance. They (the journalists) operate with one glaring premise. On the one banner that reporters wear like a gold cross around their necks is written…"*the Public has a right to know.*" This misguided, insanely silly line has given journalists the right to probe, embarrass, speculate, reveal government secrets, tap into someone's cell phone and Email, and ruin people's lives.

Of course, journalists need to pursue criminal behavior and they need to pursue every angle and probe the depths of information behind the story. But do they have to relish their work like a pit bull working on a bone? I don't know. Maybe they do. Whatever answer I come up with, there is a chorus of defense that rattles back 150 years…and will continue to rattle another century into the future. It is just what journalism does and will always do. But what is really interesting…is when they go after one of their own.

I remember that as a boy and lover of various comic books I came across an adventure story in the Yukon that has an enlightening revelation into the journalistic industry. A young man, slow afoot from an accident he had suffered earlier in the day, was trying to make it back to his camp where there was safety and shelter. He was within 100 yards when he encountered a pack of hungry wolves that stood between him and his security.

Some of the details are lost in the telling but as I remember the story the man had no weapon but did have some steel shavings and a chunk of raw meat. (Don't ask me how, why or where he got 'em) He put the shavings in the meat and tossed it to the lead wolf. The resulting injury to the mouth and throat of the wolf brought a generous loss of blood that immediately captured the attention of his faithful companions. Since they were already hungrier than a baby missing its midnight feeding, they straight away attacked the leader of their pack. The young man made a run for it, away from the distracted wolves, and safely made it to his home base. Granted, there are a few parts of the story missing but the point is…vicious animals will turn on their own when blood is flowing. It's a sad commentary but journalists are not much different. More than almost any other industry the competition is so keen between news facilities that every stumble, every lapse of strength, every wrong fact by producers and reporters are pounced upon by fellow journalists. All of them live in a glass house so it's a matter of who pounces first.

Enter and pity the news organization that screws up a breaking story involving a big personality or issue. Honor among thieves does not apply to members of the fourth estate. If a fellow competitor starts to bleed from the mouth, others are only too happy to finish him off. Case in point; CBS aired a story on a document belittling the President of the United States in the heat of a presidential campaign. An un-named source and a failure to verify a memo written by a deceased colonel who questioned President Bush's record with the National Guard was a catalyst for just about every news gatherer in the country to jump on the back of the venerable CBS anchor Dan Rather. As it turned out, Rather was using information churned up by his producer. For this exercise it is unimportant that CBS was right or wrong. It goes back to the Dung Beatle convention where the guy with the biggest dung ball had to admit he had put a marble in the center to get a head start. Rather apologized for his network but the damage had been done. ABC, NBC, Fox, CNN, the Internet all slightly bowed their heads, with a bogus tear in one eye to salute a fallen comrade-in-arms. One of their own got caught with his hand trying to take the cheese out of the trap when it snapped shut.

There were mixed feelings at CBS, including one from the esteemed anchor of anchors, the *'most trusted man in America,'* Walter Cronkite. He waited until Dan retired a few months later (hurried along by the Bush story) to take his shot. When it was announced that Bob Schieffer would temporarily fill Rather's shoes, Cronkite said, *"He is, to my mind, the man who, quite frankly—although Dan did a fine job—I would like to have seen him there a long time ago."* A not so subtle, left handed blow to the gut. One of the not so obscure secrets around CBS was that Cronkite was not a favorite himself among the correspondents while he was anchor. I used to listen to the correspondents who stopped by KSL and left behind a few choice words about him. As managing editor of his newscast, Cronkite had a final word on content and it is easy to see that he was in a no-win situation with the reporters but probably executed well with the viewer, in content and performance.

There is nothing more sanctimonious than someone who laments the fall of a competitor yet points out all the mistakes and makes assurances that such a thing couldn't possibly happen to him/her. As mentioned, most rules in journalism are either unwritten, made up on the spot or adjusted to fit a time and mood. CBS strengthened that attitude when they were so all fired anxious to scoop the others and air information that had not been thoroughly checked, breaking a time tested pledge (not a rule) to verify, verify. So much for their own former logo, *Experience.*

The whole process reinforces the *terrible truth* that more coverage and concentration are given a sensational piece—that doesn't affect a single taxpayer—than any of the networks will give to most other issues that do affect millions of Americans. As one Texas broadcaster put it, after listening to other reporters take turns shooting down Dan Rather, "...*Journalists trying to make the CBS blunder into the story of the decade are really doing nothing more than examining their own navel. The people,* he said, *were too busy sitting around the kitchen table worrying about their health care and any number of problems that personally affect them than to give a damn about some piddling' controversy."*

We define journalism in America
as the business and practice of presenting the news of the day
in the interest of economic privilege.

Upton Sinclair 1919

As beaten to death in the previous *Truth*, journalism, in one form or another, has always been about money. The one quirk of fate is that it doesn't wind up in the pockets of the individual journalists. You hear a lot of words connected with journalists—exploitive, hard, yellow, tabloid, unrelenting, both necessary and unnecessary evil, etc.—but you will likely never hear the word, *greed*. Ironic, because it is the manifesto of the corporate world that takes precedence over every action, every attitude, and every decision made in nearly every board room in America. Money *is* the ace, king, queen and jack of our lives.

Unless you've spent your life living in a dark cave on another planet you may be disappointed to hear that GREED, while always a factor in our lives, has risen to incredibly new heights. It has become the unrelenting and unstoppable driving force in all that we do…and it is not a pretty sight. Greed puts an ugly face on corporations and a heavy foot on those living from paycheck to paycheck. It creates frustration, fear, jealousy and desperation, almost killing the human spirit in the process. Greed threads its way through every industry and shows no sign of slowing down. Columnist Thomas Freidman discusses how the same dollar finances both sides of the wars in the Middle East. Oil companies earn billions yet hire people to work in their gas stations at minimum wage and charge fifty cents to put air in your tires. Every convenience once offered the public for free, now has a price tag. They are called *tiny profit centers*, thanks to every gung ho, fresh MBA out there looking for ways to increase his/her company's profit margin, with little regard for a public looking for an occasional break.

Remember when you didn't have to pay for a map or air for your tire at a service station? Information operators now charge a dollar and a quarter for a previously free service and then pour salt in the wound by saying they won't charge to connect the call. The list of those tiny profit centers appears to be growing everyday. Rarely will you find a company that presents a so-called courtesy that doesn't raid your wallet.

Unhappily, we accept the practices, bitch a little about them, shrug our shoulders and try to move ahead *without* answers and knowing full well that someone is making a great deal of money off of our naiveté and lack of information. Frankly, it is greed in its rawest form.

People are hurting and looking for answers. A fat cat (individual or company) —wanting to look good to the stockholders and investors—will prey upon the most vulnerable of the country's citizens…and it will likely never end. If the media could get their act together, we might become less ignorant why something is happening and what can be done about it. And don't think this is a personal rant; talk to any financial guru and you'll get an ear full. If a local reporter wasn't so busy listening to his police scanner looking for the next accident, he might try using some personal initiative and seek out answers to such shoddy but obvious business practices. It would help the viewers understand such problems and then, maybe, stay away from them.

Amazingly, with almost every truly committed reporter, money is *never* their driving force. Of course their newspaper or TV station ownerships covet money as much as Scrooge McDuck, and this often prompts them to stick their beaks where they don't belong. (Ask anyone in a TV newsroom their thoughts about the station's sales department.) The ownership's passion for money is very real; obsessively real.

Contention and controversy aside, while the good journalists are well compensated, their work and some of the gawd-awful hours they put in are *never* about the money. Good journalists will trade their grandmother for a first-rate story or some revelation. I knew a guy that slept in a cardboard box for a week under that overpass I was talking about to get pertinent information for a story he was doing. Watch a photographer under the basket at the seventh game of a world championship basketball game. He could care less how the game turns out. His camera is trained on a specific player, the fans or a coach's reaction. Getting that one picture or that one great piece of footage is a greater turn-on then a bevy of beauties running naked—male or female—around the perimeter of the court. And money was never the inspiration.

On one side of our mouth we say we're not about money, which is true. On the other we are governed by a budget and an ownership that is *all about* money. If you don't believe it, be a mouse in the corner when the general manager reads the latest rating report. As News Director, I worked for United Television out of Minnesota. The company owned stations in Minnesota, Texas and Utah, and was run by a hard numbers man.

In Utah we are both blessed and cursed by the Great Salt Lake; the *why* on both accounts is better left for another time. Running smack in the middle of the lake is a working railroad track. As happens once in a blue moon, a train jumped the rails. The news arrived at my desk while I was sitting with the station's general manager. I immediately excused myself and had the assignments desk order a helicopter to ferry our reporter and photographer to the scene. The manager returned to his office where he just happened to receive a call from the company president in Minnesota. In the course of their conversation the point was made that the news department had ordered a helicopter to cover a train wreck, failing to mention its location.

Always a bottom line man, the corporate president immediately called me from his office and directly asked me, *"What determines whether or not you order a helicopter to cover a news story?. After all, isn't the wreck close enough to drive to because it certainly isn't going anywhere?"* I answered that it was my gut and experience that told me what to do…not telling him the wreck was in the middle of a lake. Mr. Bottom Line delivered a short lecture on the importance of cutting costs and living with a budget. And topped it off by saying my gut and experience may be costing the station an un-needed expense. I then quietly told him of the approximate cost of equipping one of cars with pontoons, etc to get to the wreckage site in the middle of the Great Salt Lake. After a ten second pause, he said I could have told him the location of the wreck but upon reflection, knows why I didn't. We said our goodbyes and he didn't question an expense for the next two years.

Part of a reporter's arsenal is a healthy dose of cynicism. Journalism, however it is defined, is not an exact science. Far from it. More than anything it has evolved and as such, has many faces, some attractive and beneficial, others ugly as an Idaho toad and just as hard to digest. The face I remember most was one with wide-eyed optimism coupled with fear and intimidation. It is generally reserved for young, dumb, naïve reporters.

When I was a rookie in the reporting field I would be lying if I didn't admit to looking for moments of glory. Every journalist wants to get the one story that will elevate his/her status. Years ago, more time than I care to think about, I had heard that Dr. Edward Teller, the Father of the H-bomb, was between planes at the airport. A friend, who had spotted him drinking a cup of

something or other in a coffee shop, called me in the newsroom. Being eager but very inexperienced and extremely impressionable, I grabbed a photographer and left for the airport. It would be my first interview with someone of national stature.

I had remembered that something had happened in the world that day that had some nuclear ramification. What better man to ask than the one who knew more about nuclear energy then just about anyone on the planet. A comment from him would make my day and my chest would be puffed for a week. I wanted to be very professional and ask no-nonsense tough questions to show him I meant business. Truth was, I was scared to death and not real sure of the right questions to ask. In my early days in the business I instinctively knew that I had to be serious, professional…and at least look like I knew something about the subject to be discussed. The disturbing fact was that my knowledge of nuclear energy would fit into the navel of a flea but I couldn't let anyone know, especially Teller.

Arriving at the airport, my photog and I went directly to the coffee shop and, frankly, was surprised to find him still sitting there, unattended by anyone and completely anonymous to those sitting around him. Bravely, I sidled up to him and quietly asked if I could ask him a few questions, on-camera. He told me to give him five minutes and he'd meet us outside the terminal. We lost no time going to the curb to set up our equipment. I girded up my loins and waited for Dr. Teller, feeling a sweat coming on. He arrived in the time he stated and without so much as a nod, I quickly and not too delicately stuck the microphone in his face and launched into the first and only question.

At the time I thought the question was a solid query, with a tough edge, thought provoking, penetrating, original, and of course being asked by someone who was well experienced in these situations and was, of course, *professional* to the max. But reporter confidence has a way of slipping through the cracks when the interviewee is also *prepared* to the max. Actually, this man was *born* prepared. Teller paused briefly and then asked a question in return that indicated he had been down this path many times before and wasn't about to humor a reporter fresh out of day care. *"Young man,"* he said in a condescendingly kind voice, *"You want a 15 second answer, 30 second answer or a 60 second answer."* I felt my ears meeting somewhere in the middle of my head while my mind tried to grasp the gravity of the moment. I felt the features on my face disintegrate and my hand start to shake. I managed to mumble, *"30 seconds."* He said then that I'd better run the full thirty seconds. If not, then he would give me the 15-second answer. But whatever length was agreed upon, it better damn well run as given. By now, I was a wreck. Working in my parent's Texaco station in Saco was looking good.

I did know that the person being interviewed couldn't dictate terms…but I was so intimidated that I wasn't so sure of anything. I was so rattled by now I wasn't sure *what* I wanted. I didn't know what the producer of the newscast wanted and I had no idea what my follow up question was going to be. By now my head was spinning like Linda Blair's in the Exorcist. Dr. Teller must have thought I was on assignment from some local grade school paper and so thought he'd save my ass when he said., *"I'll give you both 15 and 30 second sound bites."* We filmed it, though I hardly heard a word, worrying that I didn't wet myself or drop the microphone on his foot. A second question was *out* of the question. I quickly thanked him and somehow made my way to the car, leaving the poor photographer to gather up and carry his own gear. I was too far-gone to even repeat my own name much less do something responsible. All ended well, however. The substitute for the regular film processor incorrectly mixed the chemicals and the film was destroyed in the lab. So much for the Father of the H-bomb. He deserved better…on several levels.

I got better at interviewing over the years—I better damn well get better—and in time interviewed people from all walks of life and have drawn many impressions of people and their responses. One of my favorite questions and subsequent answer was with the president of J. C. Penney. However, I was only the cameraman. After discussing the need for cooperation between retail outlets, he was asked a personal, but honest question by our reporter, Spence Kinard, that I think not only tested the man's mettle and honesty but was also a question on the lips of every viewer. His answer not only illuminated his ability to think on his feet but displayed a unique loyalty to his company and confidence in its product.

The written word does not do the exchange justice, and therein lies the true beauty of TV news. Also included were the looks on the faces of both and the way the question and answer were delivered. Both men changed expressions as if hoping for something beyond the mere give and take between reporter and subject. The suit worn by the J.C. Penney president had the look of a very expensive, well-tailored article of clothing, suitable for Donald Trump on his best day. With an appropriate amount of respect, curiosity and professionalism in his voice, Spence—with a slight twinkle in his eye—delivered the only question that was remembered by the viewer, the reporter and the respondent twenty years later.

"Are **you** wearing J.C. Penney clothing?"

…and the subject paused for just a dramatic second as he leaned forward, with a slight but confident smile, to slowly and precisely convey the answer, giving each word proper emphasis.

"Every…stitch!"

It was a moment the newsroom and the viewer enjoyed immensely. Every reporter wishes all the answers to the questions asked over the years were just as definitive. It was one of those rare times that nothing could or should be added.

Among the most difficult dimensions to understand about the media are those infrequent times when the viewers and readers are subjected to the arrogance and hypocrisy of the media. It's nothing to be proud of….but, when the media relish the idea of a story that has nine lives, even in the face of fading public interest, the media will continue to stoke those fires that first brought it to the attention of the public in the first place. Every effort is made to keep it a "current" story. Of course the question is how many lives is enough to call it quits. Depending on the subject matter there is such a thing as beating a dead horse, an action at which local TV news is very adept.

Controversy played out on a television newscast rarely has any consequence except for entertainment value. The one factor the news media forgets or doesn't wish to acknowledge is that it creates the controversy by presenting an attractive forum and then blames others while maintaining aloofness. If there is an interesting angle to a story and has the visual to go with it, it is amazing how proficient television has become at keeping it alive. If it wasn't for TV News stirring the pot, there would be less controversy and confusion over half the ongoing stories the viewers are told are terribly important, when in truth if TV news hadn't stuck its head in the door the stories would have died a natural death or perhaps never have been born in the first place.

Once committed to a story, journalists cannot just let it go once it has given it air to breathe, space in which to exercise and expand and an audience they think is hanging on every word. When interest in the story begins to wane, the journalist will too often prop it up or give it mouth-to-mouth resuscitation or add a few outside support systems for nourishment. All this when burial was called for days before or when an audience's interest or imagination had had enough, if it ever had any to begin with….

> *Journalists aren't supposed to praise things.*
> *It's a violation of work rules almost as serious*
> *as buying drinks with your own money or absolving the CIA of something.*
> P.J. O'Rourke

He's right!   Praising things is not what a reporter does. Now, that is not to say journalists, electronic or print, don't recognize valor and heroic deeds; quite the contrary. But to just go and find something to praise, out of the blue, is not in a journalist's bag of tricks. Viewers and readers of media observations have complained that nothing positive is ever reported. It is…and frankly, quite often, but the negative has more punch. Sorry, but being positive is not the nature of the industry, never has been, never will be. Even when there is not a lot to report, that is when a reporter is at his most dangerous. They know that if he turns over enough rocks, something will pop up. And it won't always warm the cockles of your heart.

When news in general dies down—meaning if it is the same old thing every day, even if a war is going on—you can bet there are reporters out there looking for something, anything. Iraq got to be so commonplace to journalists that they readjusted their antenna to pick up on other hot spots in the country, or the world for that matter, especially Afghanistan. They particularly like the continuing buzz in Washington, a veritable septic tank of juicy information. And they generally find what they want. And then they get all energized about it and before you know it, everybody is on the chase and someone's bare butt is hanging out to be blistered by the media.

196

The public at large becomes a bystander as journalists rise to the occasion of their calling. As tragic as it was, the gulf oil spill may have been a living hell for several states and thousands of people but it was heaven sent for the media. Viewers saw the best and worst reporting on the planet. Everyday there was a new story to tell so if it wasn't great reporting on one day, the journalist still had the next day to do it right. n the spring of 2006, there was one of those slow news periods where not a lot was going on to get too excited about. There were still people dying in Iraq but even that was becoming routine to the media but certainly not to the people it affected. But still, there was that lull before the storm. And then a man, indicted by a federal grand jury, said that the President had authorized him to leak classified information on Iraq to reporters.

Because surveys indicated there were falling percentages of people approving the President's job performance, the new information was the whip cream and cherry to the top of a so-so dessert the media had been munching on for over a year. The same information had had its run but now with the new revelation that it may have been the President himself who authorized the leak, there was fresh meat to chew on. Before anything could be proven, it was front-page news in the newspaper and a lead story on network news. Never mind that it didn't affect anyone in particular—the damage had already been done—but the fact that it may have been the President who did the deed, all bets were off and journalists were riding high in the saddle again and riding through previously dry streams that were now filling with refreshingly cool waters. Life was good.

Ironically, there are times when the news media have been the one influencing factor in what is being decided and how people conduct themselves because of the media. The late CBS Correspondent George Herman once recalled a loud and boisterous meeting where there was argument and dissension on all sides. And the longer the meeting dragged on the more confusion and controversy were being created. When Herman and his cameraman had had enough, they turned off their camera lights and packed up. Thirty seconds later the meeting itself came to an abrupt halt, the participants shook hands and said they'll work with each other to resolve the differences. The audience sat stunned, wondering just what the hell had just taken place the past hour. Herman commented that it was amazing how his camera and lights could both start and stop a battle of wits between combatants.

TV News is not above gossip, though thankfully, it is more relegated to the tabloids. When dealing with celebrities there is a shift in the planet's axis when it comes to describing the finer and more positive points of journalism. No one can deny that the public has a fascination with famous people and what they are doing or how they are acting, but it has no place on a television newscast. Still, if a famous person does something stupid or outrageous that an average Joe may do everyday of his life, you can bet it will make the news. Thankfully, most of it stays in the tabloid edition, but not always. But if a senator or governor slips on a banana peel it will dominate for days. And if this same married senator or governor is with his girl friend at the time…his career is over.

President Gerald Ford was often criticized for not being able to walk and chew gum at the same time. The reputation came when the President fell down some steps exiting from Air Force One and later was caught tripping again by the ubiquitous cameras. In truth, President Ford was reasonably graceful, having been a collegiate football player in his youth. But once a label has been slapped on someone, the media will never forget or forgive.

There was a time when indiscretions were ignored by the media. It was fodder for journalists around the water cooler. And then the dam broke. A Washington big shot was caught swimming in the Washington D.C.'s Tidal Basin with a stripper. It was too good to ignore and forever more everyone was fair game.

> *Journalists are unable, seemingly,*
> *to discriminate between a bicycle accident*
> *and the collapse of civilization.*
> *George Bernard Shaw*
> *1931*

And now it looks like we're coming full circle in our story about local TV news. Civilization is still thriving, no matter how hard we make it sound and look like it's collapsing. Anyone who suggests otherwise knows the spirit of the American people. The news media will continue to probe, with the enthusiasm—and hopefully, the skill—of a proctologist

I didn't really say everything I said.
Yogi Berra

A quotation in a speech, article or book
is like a rifle in the hands of an infantryman.
It speaks with authority.
Brendan Francis

Journalists, especially, love a good quote and over the years they've had a ball with Yogi Berra. But they also recognize that, as Francis writes, that a good quote can stop someone in their tracks. Reporters will sit for hours trying to find just the right one to bring a story home. If they're lucky it can be used to lead a newscast, use as a promotion, or be the basis for an entire report. If they don't hear a good one, they'll reach back into the annals of previous interviews and pull out one that is relevant to a current story. During the Iraqi crisis, an old 1898 quote from William Randolph Hearst was pulled out of the dust bin so many times that the Hearst family should be getting royalties.

Initially, Hearst wanted the U.S. to be in a war with Spain, thinking it would bring about the annexation of Cuba. To build his case, he sent photographers and reporters to Havana to confirm the rumors of war and Spanish carnage. One of his photographers, artist Frederic Remington, wired him saying, *"There is no war. Request to be recalled."* Hearst, certainly not one to be put off, cabled back, *"Please remain. You furnish the pictures. I'll furnish the war."* The next century of journalism had a field day with the quote. Pro-war protagonists have it on the first page of their go-to-war bible. The problem is, the quote was probably never uttered by Hearst in the first place, but it was just too good to resist. No one has ever found proof of its existence or found the cables themselves. Even Hearst denied saying it. *(*What he did say was ...*"You can crush a man with journalism."*) But who cares whether he said it or not. It has a legendary sound about it. As John Ford, the film director, once said, *"If legend conflicts with the truth, go with the legend every time."* What the story about the quote does say, according to writer Brendan Nyhan is that *it is an example of the media's power to propagandize and inflame public opinion on the subject of war.*

Ninety percent of the time, stated comments in the media annoy more than they anger. And fortunately, or unfortunately—depending on where you're seated—the public isn't always aware or interested that the media, mostly TV News, started something that becomes a part of the national consciousness, or at least puts it in our mind long enough to dredge up and use it in a conversation. There are always exceptions, of course. The mere way in which something is presented has an enormous influence in the public perception of an individual or event. Tape being shot at an inopportune time for the subject, or a question being answered by some unsuspecting interviewee…all are part of the extraordinary makeup of both the human tragedy and comedy in this business.

TV News also has a way of taking an offhanded remark by an unknown politician or even a quiet citizen and through shear repetition can make it a part of the American lexicon. Some are flattering, some are humiliating. The offending party can cry foul and the media just yells back, *"We didn't say it, whats-his-name did."* The naked power of repeating something over and over can literally degrade a life or lose an election. A presidential candidate can say something, or be called something, or be accused of something or kidded about something…and it could wind up on the cover of Time magazine. *Then*, try and forget it.

…and you are no Jack Kennedy!
Senator Lloyd Bentsen

This cutting remark and frankly, an unfair depiction by Senator Lloyd Bentsen of Dan Quayle during a nationally televised vice presidential debate was the one line that no-one forgot. It was obviously embarrassing to Mr. Quayle who had to live with it for years. And then, just as a new generation was maturing and the line was just a fading memory in the past, Senator Bentsen died and every television news program reminded the viewers, young and old, of the line and once again, Quayle had to relive it, yet he had nothing to do with it in the first place. But that's the media. It never forgets, regardless of who is hurt, humiliated or affected. Would I have used the line? Of course. It's what the media does. And it doesn't end there.

One description of news that tends to be forgotten is that it can perpetuate a lie, a truth, or a story, to keep it in the public eye. It may have long since lost its news appeal, but in terms of describing something or breathing life into an old blunder, there is no power like the potency of the media. Lust in Jimmy Carter's heart—a throw-a-way line to a reporter leaving his home after an interview— stuck around for weeks. No one remembers what Carter said in the earlier interview, or for that matter, the rest of the campaign but they will never forget that quiet comment on his front lawn as he walked the reporter to his car.

A former station manager of KSL Television bit the dust when he made a derogatory remark to a reporter about the founder of the Mormon Church as the reporter was getting up to leave. The lesson learned is that you don't say anything to a reporter in an interview or in casual conversation except answers to his questions and your name, rank and serial number. No adlibs or freelancing.

Another disturbing element is that the media has a nasty habit of reminding the viewers of both feats and foibles of individuals who were or are now in the public eye. If you happen to shoplift a pomegranate from the local A&P and ten years later happen to win the Nobel Peace Prize, you can bet your new Ferrari that in the first paragraph in the paper or the first ten seconds of the newscast, that damn pomegranate will trump the good news…now and forever more. No matter how successful an individual becomes after a long forgotten indiscretion, it's just a matter of time before it will surface again.

The media never forgets, and invariably any story about the individual, whether an obituary or participation in an event…the trouble will be printed or spoken or viewed right off the top. Rarely does an individual get a fair shot at a second chance. The media will make sure the 'full story' will be aired to illuminate every dimension of the individual. The argument is, of course, to present all the information available, good and bad. Their principle argument is that overused *"the public has a right to know"* statement, and if any decision has to be made…let John Q make it. And, of course, the story will be backed with every little tidbit, every juicy morsel, everything that could be gleaned from picking over someone's bones.

Don't wipe it off. It looks good.
…from the movie "Mad City"

When Dustin Hoffman—playing the role of a reporter, was bloodied as he stood on the outer edge of an explosion, but not injured enough to not finish his report. As he stepped in front of a camera to give an account of what happened, a trickle of blood started to cascade down his forehead. As he went to wipe it off an associate stopped him. It was a revealing and concluding moment in the movie, designed to hype the drama of the electronic journalist in the movie… and cast an accusatory eye at those who, in real life, look for ways to pump some zing into a story. It happens folks, whether we like it or not.

News creates news. In fact, an event that would normally not be newsworthy is sometimes embraced and at times even celebrated, yet it makes no-one any richer or more informed. It's something that reporters nearly wet their pants over. For instance, Mrs. John Heinz Kerry quietly told a journalist to "shove it." It was caught on tape and replayed until they were sure everyone was about to throw up. The convention which nominated her husband as the Democratic standard bearer was having a slow moment and Mrs. Kerry's remark was tailor made for scores of bored journalists. It was juicy and it was leaking out all over the place. It is the kind of non-story that bloodhounds drool over. Katie Couric asked Mrs. John Edwards about all the "controversy over Mrs. Kerry's 'shove it' remark." Considering it was the news media that created the controversy in the first place, Mrs. Edwards noted that she hoped Mrs. Kerry's convention speech with its references to the real problems of the world would get as much play as the 'shove it' comments. Of course it didn't and today hardly anyone can remember a single word of her speech.

A few times in the course of this book, I have mentioned the different kinds of journalism. The concept may be a little confusing to the average viewer who may not know exactly how to tell the difference of one from the other. When all this TV News business got started the reporting was pretty straight forward…a simple run-down of what had happened that day. Nothing fancy, a minimum of graphics, no editorials, no analysis of any kind—the *straight reporting*, nuts and bolts sort of stuff, the Who, What, Why, When, Where and How of journalism taught in the first week of journalism 101.

For instance, *Susie Jones was driving home from her, when she collided with another car at the city's intersection of 12th and Jefferson. The collision occurred at 5:30 p.m., a time when one bystander described as the worst time of the day. Ms. Jones was injured and was taken to the hospital where she is listed in fair condition.*

Over time, television slowly closed the gap of presenting information with new eyes and ears taking charge. Edward R. Murrow with his documentary of "Harvest of Shame" about migrant workers in California opened up a big door, aptly dubbed, *Investigative reporting. Investigative reporting* for example found that Suzie was actually being chased by another car driven by her ex boyfriend, causing her to lose control of her car. *Advocacy reporting* steps in when it was learned that the intersection where the accident happened was the scene of more accidents than any other intersection in town and the cause was poor maintenance on the street and that with more attention and diverting some of the city's safety budget, the street could be fixed in a week, saving lives and ultimately saving the city thousands of dollars on a monthly basis. *Feature reporting* came later when it was discovered that Suzie worked in a rehabilitation center and was responsible for helping dozens of people get back on their feet. *Tabloid reporting* popped up when it was discovered that in her spare time Suzie was a stripper and a secret girlfriend of the Mayor. Granted, every story may have a wrinkle or two but generally, on an evening newscast, straight reporting is the norm. That is not to say, however, that other types don't unfold on a newscast. Quite the contrary…but they unfold one at a time and are carefully calculated by the reporter and producer.

> *All newspaper and TV editorial writers ever do*
> *is come down from the hills after the battle is over*
> *and shoot the wounded.*
> Unknown

This is not a very flattering comment about editorial writers, but they do generally have something to say once an event is over, an event that sometimes has a leg still quivering. Editorialists and columnists can either breathe new life into an event or story, or deliver the coup d' grace. Either way, it can be done out of conviction, out of indignation, out of the need for further examination, or even out of fear. One story, about which everyone had something to say, involved a cabinet officer, a defrocked presidential aide and a bull session in the back of an airplane.

An incident was reported by John Dean, a former Nixon White House attorney, who was freelancing a story for a magazine. Dean wrote that on the flight returning to Washington following the Republic National Convention was a small group of Washington insiders in the back of the plane telling stories and a few jokes. He quoted one cabinet member (not identified in the article) who told an unflattering racist joke. Other journalists, upon reading the story, quickly researched the passenger list and found only one cabinet member listed. The journalistic community was absolutely giddy with what they had found and reported. Of course, the joke was in extremely bad taste and especially unworthy of a cabinet officer. When other journalists broke the story and editorial writers jumped on it, they instinctively knew it would cost Secretary of Agriculture Earl Butts his job, and it did, probably as fast as anyone has lost his job in government over an indiscretion. Don't think for a moment that journalists aren't, at times, judge and jury. Why do they do it? Personal reputation; getting a jump on the competition; approval from superiors; envy of fellow journalists; a killer instinct; a dislike for the victim; survival in the industry? Or all of the above. Also the haunting question, if the journalist happened to like and respect the cabinet officer and he was the only reporter, albeit it, a new recruit to the journalistic ranks, would he have reported it? If Butts and Dean were old drinking buddies…one wonders…..

As one examines the role of journalism in our lives, it appears that two characterizations emerge, one for the daily conventional print media and another for local TV news. There are obvious time limitations on the electronic side. A full reading of an issue is difficult for a television newscast, considering other stories are waiting in line, whereby the newspaper can always add another page. TV news, on the other hand, can—with its film and video—handle accidents and unfolding minor crime stories with more flexibility and can push together more information in a shorter period of time. Only, on occasion, will the two publish and air the same stories. A lead report on TV of an accident or drug bust one evening will receive little or no mention in the morning paper or, at best, possibly a small mention buried on the back page, thereby giving a differing emphasis to the importance of the stories. Of course, on the big stories, all bets are off. Everybody goes to the max.

The CQ (curious quotient)
plus the PQ (passion quotient)
trumps the IQ (intelligence quotient) every time..
Thomas Freidman
Columnist and Author (The World is Flat)

The best columnist in the country reminds us of the incredible life altering contributions made by those who may not be the brightest apple on the tree but have the curiosity and passion to survive and take us along for the ride. They are adept at finding solutions, utilizing appropriate energy, seeking where others fear to tread, not blinking in the middle of a confrontation, remembering what the goals are, using peripheral vision and recognizing the value of every step taken.

CQ and PQ can be particularly effective for journalists. Throughout the book, the *passion* and *curious* quotients have been discussed. It is a triumph for those who have them and regrettable for the majority who don't. When information is sought, found, and presented, the viewers will recognize those journalists *who* possess these qualities and turn away from those who fall into a reporting routine, those *who* do just enough to get by, *who* are lazy, *who* don't continually school themselves about their community, *who* forget who is watching them, or *who* forgets the nobility of their profession, no matter how high their *IQ* might be.

As stated, we live in a world of turmoil and crisis so it is natural and necessary to be reminded how bad things are in our world or our community. We also have to endure news that does not really affect our lives. We accept news that is nothing more than a series of pretty pictures. And we tolerate news that is not news however you define it.

We are sick of newscasts giving precedence to accidents and crime stories. We're not just talking and writing about the "good news" around us, that we all know is not generally the role of a journalist. We're asking for more energy, more creativity, and more investigations into those areas of our culture that impact our lives. And we need assistance to lessen our struggles in trying to more fully understand our community and how we can fill our heads with information that reach beyond the mundane, the frivolous, the unnecessary, the shallow and the self serving.

We need more TV journalists to get off their derrières and seek those stories that illuminate more than they entertain or be "chewing gum" for the eyes. And when they do find stories that genuinely affect us in one way or another, it would be a great advantage to give serious consideration to airing them all year long and not just during the rating sweeps.

In the end, we know there is very little viewers can do, short of switching channels. We know that there is a little bit of show biz in every TV newscast, that the public is fickle and lazy (when it comes to TV viewing), that news is a business with stockholders who insist on performance, and that advertisers want the biggest bang for their buck. We also know that viewers are looking for answers and that the *Terrible Truths*, whether we embrace them or not, need to be examined and exposed.

Sometimes the electronic journalism profession is so complex, the ideas so challenging, the pressure so great, the attitude so presumptuous, decisions so arbitrary, support so fragile, professional progress so slow and acceptance so brittle, it's a wonder that anyone would decide to become a journalist. And yet, those who stick with it will likely, in time, encounter the highest level of professionalism and the enormously satisfying sensation of contributing to the people's bank of knowledge. Further, they may participate in the exposure and removal of some cancer in the community, or illuminate some need to enhance the quality of a neighborhood. Even on a day-to-day basis, they will assist in deciphering verdicts, pronouncements and judgments made by officials on behalf of the people. It is a profession that demands only the best men and women have to offer. Frankly, most are not up to the challenge. For all journalists, their duties can be as difficult as a three cushion shot…but can also be just as rewarding if everything lines up correctly.

Nothing will happen overnight. It's a slow, bewildering process but people need the information that will help them understand their world and their community. But they will also have to participate in the transformation it will take to bring about a revelation that will benefit the profession and the public. So, let's all get a good night's sleep give it our best shot in the days, weeks and years to come.

Let's see. My (2 year old) grandson is defiant, inquisitive,
libelous, prone to anarchy,
indifferent to the feelings of others and
oblivious to filth.
Oh, no. He's a journalist.

Robert Kirby
Columnist

A Parting Shot!

As a twelve year old, from my lofty perch atop a tractor in Northeastern Montana, the world looked simple and plain. Never really knowing what I wanted to do with my life, I sort of made it up as I went along. Fate and some luck landed me in journalism. It was not an immediate love affair. It was a gradual courting that eventually allowed me to see more than half the world, world-class monuments, meet men and women of distinction and desperation…and rub against all the edges of my profession.

I have admitted to never standing on the top rung of my profession but I got close enough to watch, touch and listen to most of it. I feel I have had my 15 minutes and am most grateful for the opportunities. I am proud of the contributions I've made, of the stories I've covered, the documentaries and newscasts I've produced, of the way I have performed my duties. It has been quite a ride.

Behind my desk I have a picture, among others, of a country school house where NBC's Chet Huntley attended school and where years later we held country dances, the likes of which only folks tending God's green earth could truly appreciate. Chet rose to that top rung but always looked back. And as I mentioned, I finally got to meet him and we talked of Saco, the farm, people we knew, the benefits of small town upbringing. The last thing he said to me when we parted was…*"I hear they drug that old school house into Saco from my father's pasture. Is it still standing? I think of it often."* I told him it was still sitting at the town's edge. The town fathers gave it a new paint job and built two new outhouses to put in the back and renamed it "The Huntley School". Chet smiled and said, *"I could receive no finer tribute."*

Resources

1. http://www.quotegarden.com/media.html

2. http://www.foxnews.com/politics/2009/04/16/
obama-appointee-suggests-radical-plan-newspaper-bailout/

3. http://issuu.com/araujosax/docs/wiley--webster-s-new-world-essential-vocabulary--2

4. http://www.brainyquote.com/quotes/authors/b/
bob_woodward_2.html

5. http://www.poynter.org/content/content_view.asp?id=101795

6. http://www.iwise.com/David_Brinkley

7. http://famouspoetsandpoems.com/poets/g__k__chesterton/quotes

8. http://www.spu.edu/depts/history/

9. http://stodg.blogspot.com/2007/05/ah-theres-good-news-tonight.html

10. http://thinkexist.com/quotation/journalists_are_
like_dogs-when_ever_anything/297118.html

11. http://www.litera.co.uk/published_good_luck_poems/59/

12. http://uk.imdb.com/title/tt0094812/quotes

13. http://www.thenewsmanual.net/Resources/what_is_news_00.htm

14. http://www.nytimes.com/1991/07/21/movies/
jack-palance-living-the-western.html

15. http://encycl.opentopia.com/term/Foghorn_Leghorn

16. http://www.mediaonline.ba/en/arhiva/arhiva/pdf/
1999/mnbr34en.pdf

17. http://www.iwise.com/RkzWc

18. http://www.quotegarden.com/media.html

19. http://www.quotegarden.com/media.html

20. http://www.brainyquote.com/quotes/quotes/r/
robertsche346521.html

21. http://www.barrypopik.com/index.php/new_york_city/entry/i

22. http://www.facebook.com/group.php?gid=22009376

23. http://jmm.aaa.net.au/articles/4861.htm

24. http://nickelkid.net/quotes/lasorda.html

25. http://www.great-quotes.com/quote/832276

26. http://www.archure.net/minds/quotes.html

27. http://www.iankahn.com/quotations/twain.htm

28. http://mediamatters.org/print/research/200601040009

29. http://twitoaster.com/country-us/chrispirillo/whether-its-the-best-of-times-or-the-worst-of-times-its-the-only-time-weve-got-art-buchwald/

30. http://answers.google.com/answers/threadview/id/13982.html

31. http://videocafe.crooksandliars.com/heather/paul-krugman-takes-sam-donaldson-school-week

32. http://www.msnbc.msn.com/id/11960028/

33. http://www.scholarsandrogues.com/category/new-media/

34. http://books.google.com/books?id=jGbyuBwKrDMC&printsec=frontcohttp://books.google.com/books?id=jGbyuBwKrDMC&printsec=frontcover&dq=Harry+Reasoner

35. http://www.justfortheloveofit.org/inspiration

36. http://thinkexist.com/quotation/a_thing_is_right_when_it_tends_to_preserve_the/222967.html

37. http://thinkexist.com/quotes/don_hewitt/http://www.nytimes.com/2009/08/20/business/media/20hewitt.html?pagewanted=3&_r=1

38. http://www.brainyquote.com/quotes/authors/h/henry_fielding.html

39. http://www.tompeters.com/dispatches/branding/

40. http://www.financialexpress.com/news/formula-for-success-r

41. http://www.notable-quotes.com/j/journalism_quotes.html

42. http://www.nytimes.com/keyword/john-chancellor

43. http://www.originalsbymiles.com/quotes/quotes.html

44. https://www.cia.gov/library/center-for-the-study-of-intelligence/csi-

45. http://www.huffingtonpost.com/harry-shearer/whats-the-road-to-hell-pa_b_14195.html

46. http://www.squidoo.com/billmoyers

47. http://www.goodreads.com/author/quotes/61745.Eric_Sevareid

48. http://www.guardian.co.uk/media/greenslade/2010/feb/02/conde-nast-magazines

49. http://www.people.ubr.com/celebrities/by-first-name/d/dan-rather/dan-rather-quotes/hea

50. http://thinkexist.com/quotation/passion_is_the_element_in_which_we_live-without/146407.html

51. http://en.wikipedia.org/wiki/Today_(NBC_program)

52. https://myaccount.nytimes.com/auth/login?URI=http://select.nytimes.com/2006/04/05/opinion/05dowd.html&OQ=_

53. http://www.msnbc.msn.com/id/3032619/

54. http://library.umkc.edu/spec-col/ww2/pacifictheater/home-front.htm

55. http://www.memorable-quotes.com/mahatma+gandhi,a46.html

56. http://www.phnet.fi/public/mamaa1/quotesnf.htm

57. http://petcaretips.net/foghorn-leghorn.html

58. http://petcaretips.net/foghorn-leghorn.html

59. //www.actionext.com/names_k/keith_toby_lyrics/beer_for_my_horses.html

60. http://www.brainyquote.com/quotes/authors/a/arthur_h_sulzberger.html

61. http://www.basicfamouspeople.com/index.php?aid=2107

62. http://www.seattlearchdiocese.org/Assets/PS/529_StewardshipQuotes.pdf

63. http://thinkexist.com/quotation/we_live_in_a_newtonian_world_of_einsteinian/167804.html

64. http://www.facebook.com/topic.php?uid=67285055849&topic=10954

65. http://hansard.millbanksystems.com/lords
/1962/jul/18/the-pilkington-report-on-broadcasting

66. http://www.buzzle.com/articles/photography-quotes-and-sayings.html

67. http://johnstodderinexile.wordpress.com/category/writing/

68. http://www.famousquotes.me.uk/quotes-about-life/
quotes-about-tv.htm

69. http://www.livedash.com/transcript/
dance-a-lot-robot-(the_fire_truck_dance)
/4896/DISNP/Sunday_November_7_2010/330001/

70. http://www.middleweb.com/Supposedtobehard.html

71. http://www.frankwbaker.com/advertising1.htm

72. http://www.quotelucy.com/occupations/tv-news-quotes.html

73. http://www.tivocommunity.com/tivo-vb/showthread.php?t=395788

74. http://www.stateofthemedia.org/2005/narrative_localtv
_conclusion.asp?cat=8&media=6

75. http://www.leatherneck.com/forums/showthread.php?t=40498

76. http://thinkexist.com/quotes/ring_lardner/

77. http://www.globalissues.org/article/163/media-in-the-united-states

78. http://thinkexist.com/quotation/there_ain-t_no_answer-
there_ain-t_gonna_be_any/206501.html

79. http://www.memidex.com/journalism+print-media

80. http://www.yourdictionary.com/news

81. http://www.quotationspage.com/quotes/Edward_Wallis_Hoch/

82. http://www.nirach.com/

83. http://www.freerepublic.com/focus/fr/1061653/posts

84. http://www.quotationspage.com/quote/33023.html

85. http://www.imdb.com/name/nm0004847/news?year=2005

86. http://www.wordiq.com/definition/Dan_Rather

87. http://pressinamerica.pbworks.com/w/page/

18360241/Upton-Sinclair

88. http://www.quotegarden.com/media.html

89. http://www.quotegarden.com/media.html

90. http://www.quotedb.com/quotes/1322

91. http://www.quotationspage.com/quote/26778.html

92. http://www.disclose.tv/forum/10-false-flags-operations-that-shaped-our-world-t34706.html

93. http://www.disclose.tv/forum/10-false-flags-operations-that-shaped-our-world-t34706.html

94. http://www.pbs.org/wgbh/amex/kane2/

95. http://en.wikipedia.org/wiki/The_Man_Who_Shot_Liberty_Valance

96. http://www.spinsanity.org/post.html?2003_03_09_archive.html

97. http://en.wikipedia.org/wiki/Senator,_you're_no_Jack_Kennedy

98. http://www.subzin.com/s/The+wrong+way!+%3FWrong+way/8

99. http://www.fanfiction.net/u/1071336/Idiots_Unite

100. http://wenchwisdom.blogspot.com/2006/07/cq-pq-iq-flat-world-math-formula.html

101. http://www.greaterthings.com/Humor/KirbyClassics.htm

101. http://www.greaterthings.com/Humor/KirbyClassics.htm